YOU CAN LEARN TO RELAX

A PRACTICAL METHOD FOR QUIETING THE MIND

Dr. Samuel W. Gutwirth

Foreword by Melvin Powers

1974 EDITION

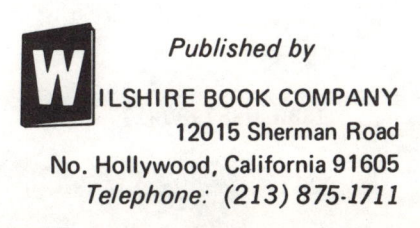

Published by
WILSHIRE BOOK COMPANY
12015 Sherman Road
No. Hollywood, California 91605
Telephone: (213) 875-1711

Copyright © 1957 by Samuel W. Gutwirth. Copyright under International Copyright Union. Manufactured in the United States of America. Library of Congress Catalogue Card Number 57-7394

Printed by
HAL LEIGHTON PRINTING CO.
P. O. Box 1231
Beverly Hills, California 90213
Telephone: (213) 346-8500

ISBN 0-87980-177-8

To
the memory of
BESS GUTWIRTH

FOREWORD

Modern man is fighting a losing battle with his emotions.

The mounting sale of tranquilizers, sedatives and other "happy" pills affords dramatic evidence that millions of individuals are failing to cope with their environment. Despite billions of dollars spent on these drugs, the results are not commensurate with the money expended, and hospitals and sanitariums become continually more crowded with the mentally and emotionally ill, who have attempted to alleviate the worries, tensions and anxieties which beset them by chemotherapy and shock treatment.

Dr. Samuel W. Gutwirth, in this book, has written a drugless prescription for those millions of individuals who are helping to make modern society the most neurotic (and psychotic) period in the history of man. It is axiomatic that man, so long as he is possessed of an imagination, will never be completely free from worry — nor is it likely that he was meant to be. History reveals that primitive man had worries in abundance, but there is no indication that he was overwhelmed by them. Yet modern man, at least a majority, seems unable to solve even the commonplace problems of everyday life, and the ability to adjust to unavoidable stress seems beyond his capacity.

It is true that the usual anxieties which affected all periods of our civilization have been compounded by the fear of the unknown — the fear that a man thousands of miles away may give the command that will destroy all civilization as we know it today. This is a very real worry and consciously or unconsciously affects us all, but if man is unable to adjust to the ordinary tensions of our culture, it is certain he will never be able to live in serenity with the problems engendered by our present tense international situation.

It is Dr. Gutwirth's contention that learning how to overcome the domestic fears which affect us every day is a prerequisite to achieving a measure of success to the deadly fear of instant annihilation. To this end, he has written a series of simple techniques of relaxation which involve control of the muscles and nerves of the body.

He is thoroughly familiar with the centers of nervous strain and how they can be utilized by normal persons to live in peace and harmony. His thesis is scientifically sound and has proved to be effective in thousands of cases.

Through autogenic training, Dr. Gutwirth shows how you may concentrate on relaxing a single area of your body at a time, working up to a point where you can attain complete relaxation in a relatively short period of time.

With hypertension and coronary disease among the chief killers, there is no doubt you can extend the length and enjoyment of your life by using his methods. As Dr. Gutwirth points out, relaxation in this age of anxiety is literally a matter of life and death.

This book should be read by everyone who is subject to the stress inherent in our modern civilization—and this includes practically all of us.

Melvin Powers

12015 Sherman Road
No. Hollywood, California 91605

Preface

EVER SINCE worrying became a characteristically human trait, man has sought through various devices to free himself from this harmful habit. More and more we are recognizing the fact that prolonged and excessive worry and fear produce disease, since they bring about well-defined physiological changes in the body.

The literature relating to the problem of worry is very extensive. In view of the great number of books dealing with this subject, what justification can one offer for placing another volume on the market, and how does it differ from all others in the field?

First of all, we must clarify one point. The contents of this book will not be concerned with theories but with facts—facts based upon many years of scientific research.

The reasons for writing this book are many. However, I shall present only the most important. Until now man has searched but has not found adequate relief from worry and fear. His failure can be attributed directly to his wrong approach toward controlling this phenomenon, since he has not taken into account the psycho-physiological processes involved in worrying.

The scientist has finally solved the enigma of the worrying process. Therefore, we can now attain our goal of controlling and eradicating worry and fear through precise methods. The procedures we outline here differ from former approaches in that these are no less logical, yet are practical and clinical rather than mere philosophical or popular.

This scientific approach to peace of mind is based upon the momentous experimental discovery made in 1929, by the renowned physiological psychologist Dr. Edmund Jacobson, to the effect that all mental activity requires an accompanying physical activity somewhere in the body; that no mental activity is possible without some muscular contraction.

The process of thinking and worrying does not occur in the mind alone, as most people believe. We have specific evidence that thinking and worrying take place in both the *brain and the muscles!* Hence worrying can be eliminated by getting rid of muscle tension. The method for bringing this about is called "progressive relaxation," which is widely approved and prescribed by the medical profession.

Muscles participate in all mental and emotional activities. Worry, fear, anxiety and other states of feeling exist not in the brain alone, but as patterns called "residual tension"—that is, muscle contractions or the tension which continues even after one thinks he has relaxed his muscles.

By learning to relax residual tension one can gain a large measure of control over the mind and the emotions. *When one discontinues tensing the muscles involved in worry, he will no longer be worrying. In short, it is impossible to be relaxed and worried at the same time.*

Man has hitherto acted largely in obedience to his instincts and emotions, less often to his reason. Now, while it has been universally agreed that dependence on reason is desirable, we must emphasize the fact that only in a relaxed state is one able to think and reason clearly. As long as the body remains tense through wrong muscular habits, conventional therapeutic methods which do not include physiological relaxation, will be only partly successful, if at all, since they fail to remove the basic cause.

Training in progressive relaxation enables the individual to

Preface

observe his own bodily sensations, by observing his states of muscular tension, when he is faced with daily problems and making adjustments to environment. When faced with difficulties and pressures, he will resort to reason instead of worry. He will be able to distinguish between a rational understanding of the issue involved and an attitude of tension. The door for a new way of living will thus be open to him. His mind will be at peace.

SAMUEL W. GUTWIRTH
Chicago, Illinois

Contents

	PREFACE	vii
1	LEARN TO LIVE	1
2	THE LEGION OF THE WORRIED	5
3	SCIENCE SHEDS LIGHT ON THE PHENOMEON OF WORRYING	10
4	TENSION, RELAXATION, AND RELATED PHENOMENA	19
5	A NEW CONCEPT OF MAN IN ACTION	32
6	THE AIM OF SCIENTIFIC RELAXATION	37
7	TECHNIQUE OF GENERAL RELAXATION	41
8	TECHNIQUE OF DIFFERENTIAL RELAXATION	63
9	RELEASE FROM WORRY AND FEAR	77
10	FOR YOUR HEART'S SAKE — STOP WORRYING	84
	GLOSSARY	97
	BIBLIOGRAPHY	103
	INDEX	111

1
Learn to Live

It is a reasonable assumption that you are interested in this volume because you are a worrier. Your habit of worrying may be occasional or constant, and may be accompanied by mild or distressing physical symptoms, for it is well established that there is scarcely a disease known to man that worry cannot create and continue. The conclusion is inescapable—in order to live a full, rich and useful life, *you can and must free yourself* of this devastating habit!

In the human race one of the fundamental urges is self-preservation (obtaining food, and securing protection against environmental dangers). As far as laboratory studies can determine, one of the major differences between man and the experimental animal (such as the dog, the guinea pig, the monkey, etc.) is that in man the process of worry springs from the struggle for existence in a society which constantly stresses the pursuit and conservation of material resources—with very little emphasis upon preserving human resources. This striving, in more nearly biological terms, is the basic drive to get ahead. It is obvious that in man, in addition to the elemental urges (self-preservation and preservation of the race), there is the added motivation to achieve personal success. This effort varies greatly among different cultures and peoples, depending largely upon the tempo of life and standards of living. Viewed thus, worry assumes the aspect of a cultural disorder.

In considering a specific remedy for the control and cure of the worry habit, we must take into account the whole man. Any method of treatment which does not begin with this premise or which regards the human organism only in terms of cells, tissues and organs will falter and fail. Medication and other measures which treat man as if he were a guinea pig, may alleviate the distress but will fail to strike at the root of the problem. In other words, we must not overlook the forest, seeing only the trees.

Man is self-directing, through the action of the muscles attached to his skeleton. Skeletal muscle is virtually the only tissue whereby he can move and exert force on objects constituting his environment.

All effort in man proceeds by contraction of muscle fibers. When a muscle contracts, its fibers are shortened. We have specific evidence that this applies not only to physical effort but also to what is commonly called mental effort (process of thinking). Muscular relaxation can, therefore, be considered as freedom from effort, both physical and mental.

In this volume we shall consider the terms "worry" and "fear" as being synonymous, since both produce an unhappy state of mind. There are two distinct types of fear—normal and abnormal. Normal fear helps to maintain and prolong life by teaching caution when actual danger threatens. The English philosopher, Herbert Spencer, asserted that without fear man could never have succeeded in advancing from a primitive to a civilized state. When excessive, however, fear may dominate a person's life to the extent that it interferes with normal living. Abnormal fear—fear without a basis in reality—constitutes a disease, since it burdens the nervous system and may produce disorders in other systems of the body as well.

In this volume the scientist and his laboratory unite to help the worrier control his destructive habit of worry and attain mental tranquility. The individual can surmount worry by cultivating the art of scientific relaxation as presented here,

Learn to Live

and applying it to everyday living. This ability can be acquired by anybody, at any age, by following the specific instructions presented, and through practice.

The art of scientific relaxation is based upon physiological methods, and, as stated above, the technique is learned through instruction and practice—in the same manner as one acquires such skills as golf, bowling and dancing. The purpose of training is to teach one to become aware of muscular tensions throughout the body under any conditions so that he learns to sense and recognize such tensions and cultivates the ability to let the muscles "go" under any circumstances; thus, he acquires a state of physiological relaxation. In time, this relaxation will become automatic—"second nature"—requiring little or no active attention on the part of the individual. Thus one lowers one's tension level, in contrast with previous states of irritability and excitement. In addition, one will train himself to meet conditions of stress by directly observing his *reaction attitude with the proper state of calmness.*

To stop worrying and to quiet the overactive nervous system, including the mind, you will be instructed to relax the muscles only. This prescription is based upon the fact that the tension in the muscles is the cause of your distress. Your wrong muscular habits are responsible for this tension. Through physiological relaxation, you will not only reeducate your nervous-muscular system but your emotional behavior pattern as well. You will stop worrying! Why? One cannot be worried, fearful, irritable or angry when one is fully relaxed.

By means of this scientific approach to peace of mind, you will acquire both tranquility and better health, since you will be able to manage yourself more efficiently and with less wear and tear on your body. With the elimination of such useless wear and tear, you will prevent premature senility—thus prolonging your life span!

Due to the prevalence and seriousness of coronary heart disease, the author is devoting an entire chapter to a discussion of this disorder and its relation to worry and tension. Statistics disclose that heart-and-artery disease has become the nation's Number One Killer. It now accounts for nearly 800,000 deaths a year, or one-half of the United States' total mortality figure.

Medical research finds that nervous hypertension and coronary heart disease are closely related. Therefore, as one of the essential preventive measures, it is vitally important that muscular tension be recognized and eliminated by tense individuals who may be predisposed to this disease.

It is equally important that the patient who has been stricken with a heart attack and as a result has developed organic heart injury, learn to relax so that he may preserve his heart and prolong his life. In coronary victims, scientific relaxation will bring about a calm state of mind and help to remove the anxiety which accompanies this disease. There are thousands of persons who are needlessly incapacitated through fear of experiencing another possible heart attack. The application of therapeutic relaxation can play a most important role in the rehabilitation of such persons.

In conclusion, let us emphasize that by cultivating habits of relaxed living, you will acquire a method of heart hygiene or heart preservation, whereby your heart will receive the consideration it deserves, whether it be healthy or diseased.

2
The Legion of the Worried

WE ARE now face to face with the fact that anxiety is one of the great modern plagues besetting society.

Millions, searching for tranquility, are advised and exhorted by physicians, professional counsellors, clergymen and friends, "You must stop worrying." But how many have been taught the art of controlling worry? Unfortunately, very few. So the legion of the worried grows and physical and mental suffering continue.

Man is capable of adjustment to nearly any environmental condition with which he is confronted—he can overcome almost insurmountable obstacles. Through constructive thinking he is capable of extraordinary achievement, but when he permits his thinking to fall into channels of worry and fear, he invites trouble.

Evidence from reliable sources indicates that over fifty per cent of all the illnesses physicians encounter are emotionally induced. Some authorities claim that the figure may be as high as eighty per cent. A prominent medical scientist declared recently, "Worry is the most subtle and destructive of all diseases." Worry disrupts the important systems in the body since it affects *every organ,* and the cells and tissues that make up its structure.

Persons with distressing symptoms created by worry frequent medical offices and hospitals, not realizing their illness is the result of *emotional stress,* which profoundly affects the body. *Emotional and mental strain produces physical disorders*—for it is established that mental and physical disturbances are *completely intertwined*. Worry, for example, may manifest itself in high blood pressure—or in signs of indigestion and colitis—or in countless other symptoms.

These men and women seeking help often suffer from many and varied symptoms, the most common, according to statistics, being:

1. Chronic fatigue
2. Insomnia (acute or chronic)
3. Nervousness (the author's book, *How to Free Yourself from Nervous Tensions,* covers the approach to this problem).

Typical comments from victims are, "I wake up more tired than when I went to bed," "What has happened to my energy?" or, "I would give anything if I could get a good night's sleep" or, "I am so nervous that I can't stand it much longer!"

Still others may complain of stomach pain, chronic indigestion, constipation, diarrhea, "gas" pains, a "bloated feeling" in the stomach, a "choking" sensation or a "lump" in the throat. Some may be troubled with pains around the heart, palpitation, dizziness and constant headaches. And often others may complain of pains in the back of the neck, shoulders, legs, or in the back itself. The symptoms are endless.

In most instances, after careful medical investigation, diagnosticians maintain that there is nothing wrong—at least nothing that is visible in the test tube or in the x-ray film. Nevertheless, these people are *sick!* Their complaints are real. They look sick.

Worriers are also frequently told their symptoms are due chiefly to their "overworked imaginations." They are advised to "Go home and forget it." Here again, they are seldom *shown how to stop worrying or how to forget!* Those who dismiss such sufferers in this manner should take into consideration that their solution is not as simple as it may sound. To

The Legion of the Worried

learn to *forget at will* or to stop worrying, requires certain technical training in scientific relaxation. Therefore, before such advice is rendered, the advisor must, himself, be trained in this specialized field and must know how to relax before he can teach the patient.

These patients, bewildered and in despair, may roam from one physician to another, hoping to obtain relief. Failing in this, some of these sufferers are likely to patronize quacks and pseudo-religious cults. Charlatans, well aware of this situation, use their craft to advantage by extracting millions of dollars each year from persons who have "worried themselves sick." They do not "cure" these individuals, but they do listen patiently, display interest and offer sympathy. The basic condition remains unchanged.

There is also an inclination for such sufferers to resort to various patent medicines. Such self-medication can be extremely dangerous.

These persons wonder what is wrong with them. What is this mysterious malady which produces such numerous and varied symptoms? Why does the sickness stubbornly refuse to yield to the skill of the physician and all his "wonder drugs"?

Occasionally, some functional maladies will respond to prescribed medication and the patient may obtain relief, but too often this relief is of short duration and may be followed by a relapse. Or the patient may come back complaining of new symptoms. It is obvious why this occurs—the symptoms have been treated instead of the *basic cause*.

Until the worrier confronts the etiology or source of his distress and learns how to eliminate it, he will not get well.

If your distressing symptoms are caused by your habit of worry, then application of the therapeutic measures as outlined in this book will help remedy this tendency, and as a result you will rid yourself of your suffering and avert new or additional discomforts.

However, the first step is to obtain expert medical advice.

Do not attempt self-diagnosis or self-treatment, for this is foolhardy and often self-destructive. Only a skilled physician is qualified to diagnose your condition and tell whether your difficulty is organic or functional (without organic basis).

Now to the answer—what do we find in those persons who worry? Why do they feel so miserable? The diagnosis is *tension—nervous and muscular.*

During extreme worry, general emotional upset or fear, specialized equipment in the laboratory will generally reveal varying states of high tension in any *nerve* or *muscle*. Persons who worry continuously or who are constantly over-emotional acquire a chronic condition of *overactive nerves*. By overactive nerves we mean that nerve tension is high, i.e. various nerves or muscles in the body are discharging electrochemical waves more frequently than they normally should.

Since habits of excessive muscular tension affect mental attitudes, *the worrier must learn to relax!* The individual in need of relaxation therapy must learn the art from concrete experience rather than from mere reading and discussion. *Relaxation is a physical skill, not an intellectual discipline.*

How is one to relax the nerves? To achieve this goal you need only to let the muscles "go" (application of physiological relaxation). This results in bringing quiet to the nerves, including the mind. For it is established that when muscles relax, the nerves to and from those muscles relax also. The same process is believed to occur also in those parts of the spinal cord and brain to and from which the nerves run. Muscles and nerves do not operate as units in themselves but only as elements in the nervous-muscular system. Consequently, by relaxing our muscles we ultimately relax the entire nervous system.

The relation between tension and relaxation on the one hand, and mental strain on the other, though perhaps difficult for the average person to fully comprehend, was established as

The Legion of the Worried

far back as the early part of the century by research authorities in this field. One of the most renowned authorities in this field is Dr. Edmund Jacobson, at present Director of the Laboratory for Clinical Physiology in Chicago, Illinois.

Today, as a result of extensive progress made in this science, there is a much clearer conception of the "mind" in its relation to the body and of an efficient procedure by which the average person can meet present-day difficulties. The individual who learns the art of relaxation acquires a precious skill. Fortunately, once he learns to relax he tends to retain that ability. One learns to play the violin, for example, and never completely forgets how to play it, but in order to master and maintain that skill one must practice constantly. Loss of skill is the result of lack of practice. The same principle applies to relaxation.

In concluding this chapter let us stress the fact that countless lives can be prolonged through the application of relaxation in daily living. This applies particularly to persons who suffer from organic diseases, since even in the presence of certain organic disorders, one can live and carry on a useful and happy existence if through relaxation he avoids undue worry and excitement over his condition.

3

Science Sheds Light on the Phenomenon of Worrying

THE NUMBER of disorders caused by high nerve tension in the world's population is constantly mounting. In the United States the incidence of such disorders has created a serious problem. Facilities of hospitals and sanitariums that house the nervously broken down individuals are becoming inadequate to meet the demands made on them. While there are numerous reasons for this situation, the principal cause is to be found in the strains and complexities of modern civilization.

In America, with our incomparably high standard of living and our constant striving to outstrip the rest of the world in progress—industrial, financial, educational, technological and social—we should expect to find countless minds that are overactive. High achievements are realized only after much thinking and planning. However, they also entail ceaseless pressure upon the organism. Uncertainty over the future in this atomic age has further added to mental overstimulation.

In a changing era, efforts expended daily in the struggle to exist and to get ahead not only affect a nation as a whole but wield a profound influence upon the individual. One consequence of living under pressures much greater than normal is the creation of high nerve tension and added worry. Thinking

Science Sheds Light on the Phenomenon of Worrying

and emotion may at times become so intense that the individual becomes incapable of controlling them. The question naturally arises whether anything can be done to bring about mental calmness in the presence of all this chaos. How can one adjust himself to present-day civilization without destroying his physical and mental health?

The human race has tried to relieve itself of the effects of worry by various means. There are many popular methods. Most frequently, men and women tell their troubles to persons who listen sympathetically and give advice. Very often clergymen are sought for proper guidance. Physicians advise their patients to speak freely of their perplexities and to withhold nothing. Some persons seem to find relief from heavy burdens by reading popular books of an inspirational nature, which offer formulas for attaining "peace of mind." Others seek a solution in the teachings of philosophers.

Still others try amusement and change of scene for relief from mental strain. They attempt to "divert their minds of their worries" by attending sport events and indulging in games. Some pursue cultural interests. Still others find consolation and help in reaching a balanced state of mind by living closer to nature; and some by travel and change of occupation. Unfortunately, many also resort to drugs and alcohol. And many, in the presence of excessive burdens, will try "self-control," "will power," and "determination."

The reason people resort to these various devices is the customary belief that when one worries he does so with his *mind—not* with his body. People agree, to be sure, that worry occurs within the body but hold to the mistaken concept that it occurs in a specific region, namely, within the skull. The idea likewise prevails that this is true of one's memory, attention, fears and other emotions, and, in particular, imagination. People yield to the inference that mental processes occur in the mind, and when muscles become tense this is regarded as a result or manifestation of what goes on in the mind.

The explanation for this prevailing notion is the age-old tendency to consider the mind and the body as two separate entities. The idea has become fixed as a result of traditional belief transmitted from one generation to another.

Realizing the inadequacy of the above-mentioned popular methods as therapeutic measures for the elimination of worry and harmful emotions, and the unscientific and speculative basis on which they rested, Dr. Edmund Jacobson decided many years ago (1908) to investigate this matter scientifically. It is interesting to learn how he became engrossed in this study and to present a brief survey of his achievement in this field.

While a student at Harvard University, Dr. Jacobson had the good fortune to study under the world-famed William James, Hugo Muensterberg and Josiah Royce in the Department of Psychology (which they made famous). At the same time he worked with Dr. Walter Cannon the eminent physiologist. There he began a study of the emotional phases of nervousness, particularly the measurement of certain of their effects. Reluctantly his attention was turned away from the psychological toward the physiological aspects of the phenomena under study. He found that regardless of the prior emotional state of the subject, what was called "nervousness" (within the limits of the investigation) disappeared if the subject relaxed his skeletal muscles sufficiently.

However, the psychological aspects of the study were not to be ignored. When the subject was excited, his muscles were tense and then he could note certain sensations (i.e. from the muscle spindles). Now, sensations can be regarded as signals to the organism, and those which inform a person regarding states of his body are known to psychologists as "proprioceptive sensations." He found that what laymen call the feeling of "nervousness" consists of certain proprioceptive sensations, particularly of the muscular type. If these sensations diminished toward the vanishing point, the subject (whether lying or sitting) went to sleep. If they diminished moderately, his nerves

Science Sheds Light on the Phenomenon of Worrying

calmed perceptibly. These investigations proved beyond a doubt that by "relaxation" is meant the lengthening of muscle fibers and the inactivity of nerves.

This discovery led Dr. Jacobson to create the science of relaxation, and resulted in his perfecting a method of therapy known as "progressive relaxation." The Jacobson technique for the treatment of maladies created by nervous tension, including the functional nervous disorders and insomnia, is well known throughout the scientific world.

Following these exhaustive studies, there was still a very important problem to be solved. Does muscular relaxation bear any relation to thinking, emotion, and other so-called mental activities? Investigations bearing on this problem began at the University of Chicago in 1922 and were continued there until 1936. Since then they have been conducted at the Laboratory for Clinical Physiology, in Chicago. The subjects were trained to relax, as well as to report on their subjective experiences from muscular contractions. Clinical records were made on individuals who participated in the investigations.

It has been known since 1888, during the era of Sir Francis Galton, the English scientist, that all persons necessarily use some images in their various forms of mental activity. For example, if you think of an automobile or any other concrete object, you will probably see some sort of picture of it; this picture is relatively clear in some individuals but in others is likely to be imperfect, vague and brief. Trained observers have generally agreed also that when they imagine or recall some muscular (physical) act they have an experience which seems faintly to reproduce or be comparable to what occurs during the real act. Whereas, according to reports from the highly skilled observers, individuals vary greatly in the capacity and extent to which they use these various types of imagery, it is agreed, as previously stated, that everybody employs some types of images whenever he thinks.

In the investigations, the subjects in the study, lying on

couches and properly relaxed, were at certain intervals requested to imagine or recall experiences of all sorts, and to give an accurate description of what occurs at such moments. The investigator was cautious to avoid suggesting his opinions to any subject. What the others reported was not disclosed to any experimentee. Still, they virtually all agreed that when they saw pictures in imagination or recollection they simultaneously had faint sensations as if their eye muscles were contracting to look in the direction of the pictured object. Upon relaxing the eye muscles completely, they reported that the visual images diminished or vanished.

When subjects were requested to imagine counting from one to ten or to remember the words of a poem or some recent conversation, nearly all affirmed that they felt sensations in their tongue, lips and throat as if they were actually speaking aloud, except that the feeling was much fainter and of briefer duration. Upon relaxing the tongue, lips and muscles of the throat entirely, most of them asserted that imagining or recalling the numbers or words ceased. Certain subjects were of the opinion that with relaxation of the speech organs they still saw numbers or words in imagination. However, they were in accord that there were sensations from eye muscles present at such moments. *Heeding the instruction to relax entirely the muscles of the eyes and of speech, all the subjects agreed that mental activity diminished or ceased.*

While the evidence presented above is, to be sure, incomplete and meager, it will give a general idea of the early investigations. Readers interested in a more comprehensive account will find it in a textbook written by Dr. Jacobson entitled *Progressive Relaxation*.

The likelihood of being able to determine and measure what occurs in the body at a moment of mental activity was the incentive that led to the development of electrical measurements in this field. Early apparatuses developed by others were found to be insufficiently sensitive for measuring residual con-

Science Sheds Light on the Phenomenon of Worrying

traction. In 1928, Dr. Jacobson devised and assembled equipment that recorded voltage changes in muscles as low as one millionth of a volt. More recently, muscular contractions or tension have been measured in microvolts (millionths of a volt) by means of the neurovoltmeter or myovoltmeter. Since mental operations involve muscular contractions which are *microscopic,* and so require mechanical or electrical amplification to bring them to notice, the need for extremely sensitive instruments is apparent. Thousands of records were taken measuring the speed of relaxation and residual tension. At present the measurements are taken with the integrating neurovoltmeter. Recordings are standardized in microvolts and are accurate to a fraction of a microvolt (See accompanying graphs).

These investigations provide ample evidence that mental activities, in addition to images and perhaps other elements, essentially include what might be called faint and abbreviated muscular acts. In clinical as well as laboratory studies we have sufficient evidence that with the relaxation of such muscular acts, the entire process of thinking practically stops for short periods.

A worried or mentally disturbed patient, if he has been thoroughly trained to report what takes place during moments of disturbance, says that visual images are present concerning the matter troubling him, as well as slight sensations—as from eye-muscle and other muscle tensions—while he pictures and tells himself what the trouble is about. In tests, to date, electrical devices have confirmed the presence of muscular contractions during such mental activities. With a subject who is under severe emotional strain, worry or fear, the investigator can connect his wires to any nerve or muscle and will generally find the part in a state of high tension.

In clinical practice there are two ways to rid the patient of worry and other undesirable mental activity. One is to train him in *general relaxation* (this includes the entire body lying

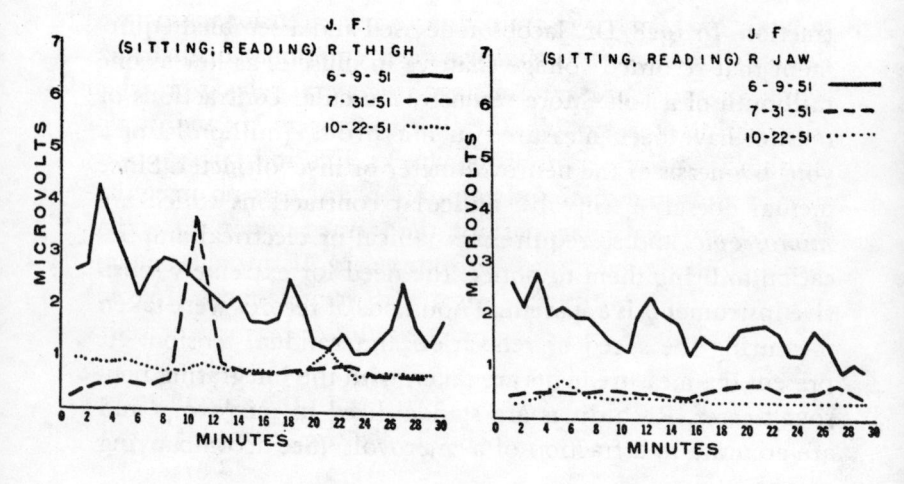

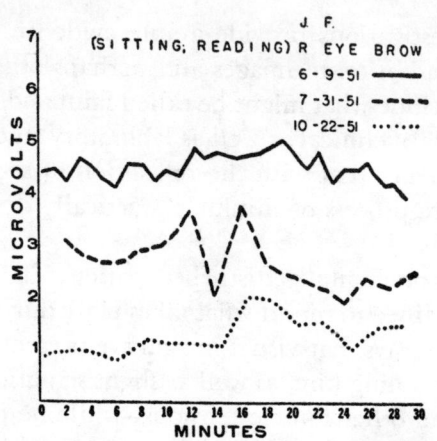

Graphs illustrate action-potential recordings taken from right thigh (above left), jaw (above right), and eyebrow (center) regions with bare wire electrodes at three different times during a course in progressive relaxation. Each tracing represents a series of integrated values over a time for a 30-minute period. The lower the microvoltage, the lesser the degree of tension in the part. Unbroken line shows initial recording, broken line recording taken seven weeks later, and dotted line is test taken three months later.

Science Sheds Light on the Phenomenon of Worrying

down); the other is to train him to relax tensions associated with the mental process of worry or emotional disturbance. One can notice at a certain stage in general relaxation when the eyeballs stop looking, the closed lids seem lax and do not wink, the entire region of the cheeks, lips and jaws, appears flaccid and quiescent, and respiration discloses no irregularity. When visual imagery stops, the trained person states that for the time being he is free from worry. If through general relaxation one can reduce disturbed mental states, it seems logical to expect that with practice almost permanent relief can be obtained.

The second procedure, namely, to train the patient to rid himself of a special or general form of anxiety, demands that he first learn to note and report his sensations with accuracy. For example, a person may constantly recall events associated with a person dear to him that he has lost through death. Or he may reproach himself for making a poor financial investment in which he lost heavily, etc. Such disturbing reflections may reach such proportions that they interfere with working efficiency and life in general. In this case the instructions are to keep the eyes open but to relax the tense eye muscles which "look at the pictures"—and, otherwise, still not stop any activity. Along with the eyes, the speech apparatus is relaxed. This is *differential relaxation.*

By way of recapitulation, it may be said that the benefits from skill in relaxation are conducive to physical and mental health. The mental aspects of relaxation were authenticated and are based upon Dr. Jacobson's momentous experimental discovery in 1929 that all mental activity requires a physical concomitant somewhere in the body—that no mental activity is possible without some muscular contraction. This discovery way duly substantiated with the development of extremely precise instruments.

Thus we have the answer to the question, what have muscle tensions to do with normal mental activities. Experiments disclose that when you imagine or recall or reflect about anything, you tense your muscles somewhere, as if you were really looking or speaking or being active, but only very slightly. If such particular tensions are relaxed, you stop to imagine or recall or reflect concerning the matter—and that includes worrying. You can achieve such relaxation while you are lying down and while you are active in your daily affairs.

4

Tension, Relaxation, and Related Phenomena

IN ORDER to obviate the necessity of devoting entire chapters to various important topics pertaining to the field of relaxation, the author presents the essence of that material in an abridged form through the medium of questions and answers.

TENSION

What is tension?
To us the term has three aspects:
1. The "tense" person is considered "high-strung," contracting his muscles needlessly. This tension is chronic—present even when he tries to rest.
2. A tense muscle is in a state of contraction; that is, its fibers are shortened.
3. Tense muscles produce a *definite sensation*. We shall call it the "tension-sense," wherever and whenever it appears in the body and whatever its intensity.

What is residual tension?
Residual tension is a fine, continued contraction of muscle along with slight movements or reflexes. It can be inwardly

observed through the sensation created by the contracting muscles.

What are the signs that reveal the presence of residual tension in an individual who lies "relaxed" in the popular sense of the term, but not entirely relaxed physiologically?

His breathing is slightly irregular in time or force and he may sigh at times. The pulse rate may be normal but is likely to be somewhat higher, as compared with later tests; the same is true of his blood pressure and body temperature. Close observation discloses that he is not perfectly quiet. He moves slightly at times, with a slight wrinkling of the forehead, rapid winking and frowning. He contracts the muscles about the eyes or moves the eyeballs under the closed eyelids, shifts his head, a limb or even a finger. The knee-jerk and other deep reflexes can be procured if no local nerve injury is present. Any sudden, unexpected noise produces a start. There is continued spasm of the esophagus and colon. Lastly, the mind continues to be active, and once the process of worrying has begun that depressive emotion tends to continue.

It may seem incredible that such a faint degree of tension can be responsible for all this. Actually the additional relaxation necessary to overcome residual tension is very slight. Nevertheless this slight advance in relaxation is exactly what is needed. As the individual relaxes past the stage of residual tension, his breathing becomes regular, the pulse rate may drop to normal, the temperature and blood pressure fall, the knee-jerk and nervous start diminish or disappear, as does the alimentary spasm, and mental and emotional activity diminish or disappear for brief periods. The individual then lies quietly with limbs flaccid, with no visible trace of stiffness anywhere, and with no reflex swallowing. For the first time his eyelids become quite motionless and attain a characteristic toneless appearance. Tremor, if formerly present, diminishes or disappears, and slight movements now stop. Subjects reporting their experiences agree that this resulting condition is both restful and pleasant. If maintained, it becomes the most restful form of natural sleep. Persons in good health and patients who have taken a course in therapeutic relaxation never consider this condition as being a suggested, hypnoidal or trance state, but a perfectly natural condition. Persons who question this are unfamiliar with the actual procedure, since their knowledge is limited by merely reading a description of this state.

SCIENTIFIC RELAXATION

What is scientific relaxation?
There is much evidence that the general public does not know the true meaning of the term "relaxation" in its relation to physical-nervous-mental well being. The average person associates "relaxation" with watching a telecast or motion picture, listening to music, playing cards, golf, drinking a cocktail, hunting, fishing, etc. To some individuals, relaxation suggests taking a vacation, and having the leisure to indulge in whatever pastimes appeal to their individual tastes and inclinations.

To a professional instructor or educator in scientific relaxation the term signifies something entirely different To him the afore-mentioned activities are amusements, recreations and diversions but not relaxation in the scientific sense. Relaxation as we wish it to be understood is much more far-reaching in its effects and more beneficial and constructive in its process; for, beginning with a purely muscular and nerve ease, it leads to a gradual re-creating of the individual. *Relaxation means physiological rest or calmness for the nervous system, and denotes the absence of tension.*

The insomniac, fatigued or nervous person is often advised by his physician to rest. His symptoms may be so annoying that he realizes rest is imperative for their alleviation. Let us consider what actually happens when he lies on a couch or bed, seemingly "relaxing." To an inexperienced observer the individual appears to be quiet, calm and "relaxed." However, he may lie there for hours or days and be nervous, sleepless and in a state of excitement. His mind may be constantly active, and worry, anxiety, and other disturbing emotions may be present. Under such conditions it is evident that his rest is not complete. Because of its inadequacy, the person often fails to receive any benefit from this type of "relaxation," and retains his symptoms of insomnia, fatigue and nervousness.

It is obvious that relaxation to an extreme degree is necessary, and must be cultivated in order to obtain the desired beneficial results. This can be accomplished through learning and applying the technique of "progressive relaxation." Progressive relaxation is a method that quiets the nervous system, including what is commonly called the "mind," by eliminating what is known as *residual tension.*

Learning to abolish residual tension is the most important feature of the course of relaxation. Only well-trained individuals who are in practice can accomplish this in a moment. In most cases it requires several minutes. Often it is reflexly excited, as by pain or distress; however even under these circumstances relaxation is to be undertaken.

Why is this method called "progressive relaxation"?

The method is called "progressive relaxation" because the learner increases the degree of relaxation gradually; because he learns to relax his muscle groups serially until he is able to relax them all simultaneously; because he advances to a stage where quiet in the nervous system is automatically maintained from day to day; and because such relaxation becomes second nature.

How does progressive relaxation differ from other types of "relaxation"?

1. It depends on the natural ability of the individual to relax his parts.

Tension, Relaxation, and Related Phenomena

2. The relaxation is carried to a more extreme degree, involving the relaxation of *residual tension*.

What are some of the proved values of progressive relaxation?

1. More effective and lasting results are obtained than through the use of sedatives, therapeutic baths, suggestion, hypnosis, the old-fashioned "rest-cure," diversions, vacations and change of scene.

2. Progressive relaxation, being free from all effort, involves no increase but rather a reduction in energy output; it is a form of self-direction which does not result in fatigue or any other harmful effect however long continued.

3. It can teach one to live without dangerous strain on his heart and blood vessels and without upsets of the digestive tract; to maintain business and social efficiency, and eliminate the wear and tear on the nervous system which is characteristic of so many in this hectic age of ours.

4. One learns to conserve energy and avert fatigue.

What are the important benefits derived from progressive relaxation?

Persons who learn the art of relaxation will reap the following benefits:

1. Maintain good physical and mental health.
2. Prolong their earning power period.
3. Maintain vitality and energy.
4. Combat infectious diseases more readily.
5. Prolong their lives.

What happens during physiological relaxation?

1. There is the complete absence of all contractions in the muscles.
2. There is a lengthening of muscle fibers as they become inactive.

3. In a person lying completely relaxed, all the "skeletal muscles" or those attached to the bones are limp.

4. During complete relaxation the tension-sense is absent.

5. During complete relaxation, the nerves present in the muscles carrying messages to the brain and from the brain are completely inactive.

Does it require high intellectual ability to learn the art of scientific relaxation?

No. A person with average intelligence can learn to relax.

Are there limitations as to age in learning the art of relaxation?

None. Relaxation can be taught to persons of all ages.

In relaxation training, why are the large muscles observed first?

The large muscle groups are observed first because the sensation occurring in them is most distinct.

Is there a difference between ordinary or natural relaxation and cultivated relaxation? Are their benefits identical?

The process of relaxation, whether natural or cultivated, is essentially the same. Their benefits are identical, as progressive relaxation is simply *cultivated natural relaxation.*

How can the therapeutic effects of progressive relaxation be explained?

In a few words, the effects of relaxation can be explained in terms of reduced excitation or lessened irritability of nerve centers.

REST

What is rest?

People commonly take rest for granted, like the air they breathe, knowing little of its physiological basis. However, rest is not so simple a matter as it may appear. For example, most persons, if asked, "What is rest?" would possibly reply, "It is what you do when you lie down." Yet, very often this is not true. An individual lying down may be very *restless;* he may turn and toss and may be so disturbed that ultimately he gets up to obtain relief! Though he may be very tired, he finds it more bearable to be up and about than in bed—he gets up in order to obtain "rest," in a sense, from lying down. During emotional upsets, some persons complain that when lying down for a prolonged period of time they become "nervous" or "get the jitters."

At first blush, these facts appear difficult to conceive—almost contradictory. Lying down seemingly should require less exertion in itself than being up and active, and consequently should be more restful. To a certain degree this is true; but the evidence already presented in this volume suggests that whether one rests adequately depends on something more than merely the posture he assumes.

According to the findings of modern science, this something is the degree of muscular relaxation. When persons lie down at night they probably do not relax most of their skeletal muscles (the muscles attached to the bones) fully and continually; relaxation will not be complete in various parts of their bodies. In other words, where this condition exists, there will be *residual tension*. The greater the residual tension and the longer it is maintained, the less complete will be the rest and revitalization.

Residual tension reveals itself through tossing and turning; by fidgeting, frowning and wrinkling of the forehead; by excessive thinking and dreaming; and it may result in such impatience that one finally leaves the bed, turns on the light and indulges in some activity.

True relaxation will be attained if one lies quietly and more or less continually in one position, yet without holding oneself still. To an observer the forehead and brow will be unwrinkled; the eyes will be almost motionless, the face expressionless; the whole demeanor will be that of restful and effortless quiet.

One should not hold himself still in attempting to relax. Such a procedure is just a useless imitation of genuine relaxation. Holding still rquires effort, with resultant fatigue. Whenever a person who lies down complains that attempting to relax makes him "nervous" or gives him "the jitters" or has not brought about "relief of tension," there is no doubt that his endeavor to relax has been carried out incorrectly: certain muscles have been contracted persistently in a misdirected effort to relax.

Why is rest so important in the treatment of disease?

In contrast to the advances in other fields of present-day medical science, nothing has been discovered to replace rest, which continues to be the most widely employed therapeutic agent in medical practice.

Obviously, the importance of rest from a clinical standpoint arises from some essential need of living matter. It is known that active movements of the organism, as well as the active maintenance of rigid or steady states require for their energy the breakdown of more complex into simpler substances. In contrast to these energizing or destructive phases within the organism, there must occur corresponding restorative processes—the rebuilding of potential energies. If action depends chiefly on the destruction of nervous energy reserves, rest can be identified as the phase of reconstruction. Doubtless this is the characteristic basis of the chemistry and physics of the human body, which accounts for the universal employment of rest in the treatment of disease.

Why is it advisable for the average adult to take periodic daily rests?

The average individual can profit from more rest than is

commonly taken in this country. Mild fatigue is usually ignored by most people; yet the best management of the organism in the maintenance and improvement of health requires more frequent rests than are generally taken.

The average adult would benefit immensely if he took an hour's rest before the noonday as well as before the evening meal. Rest after the meal is just as beneficial. In restless individuals, this habit should be acquired gradually.

INSOMNIA

What is the real cause of sleeplessness?

A person suffering from insomnia may be surprised to learn that *he* alone is chiefly responsible for his inability to fall asleep: that his habits of high nerve tension are responsible for this condition. He may attribute his insomnia to pain or illness, but even under such circumstances one should learn to be sufficiently relaxed to obtain sound sleep.

The average insomniac fidgets, fumes and frets because he cannot go to sleep. He does not realize that in doing so, he is creating a vicious circle: fidgeting hinders sleep, the insomnia in turn creates more fidgets, and this leads the insomniac to worry about his condition, which piles tension upon tension and makes sleep even more difficult. In such a state one may also worry about other matters, usually pertaining to troubles.

How to break this vicious circle? Failure to fall asleep is due to repeated shifting or moving about in order to become more comfortable. *This is doing.* Provided that a person's muscles and nerves are free from disease, he has the ability *not to do*. This does not mean that one should restrain himself from doing, for this commonly means that one holds himself quiet—which is being tense, not relaxed. Moving about in bed, seeking a comfortable position is a voluntary action performed by the individual himself; he is not compelled to do it. He does it because of his habitual tendency to make himself more comfortable or to avoid discomfort. In doing so he makes the serious mistake of creating additional muscular tension, and this in turn produces insomnia.

Attempts to overcome insomnia through effort will result in failure. The solution for this malady is to sacrifice comfort for the moment—relaxing in spite of discomfort, just simply letting go, doing nothing, ceasing activity—and only then will sleep come. As long as one attempts to relax with *effort*—which is tension—or *tries* to sleep, he will not succeed.

How can a person overcome insomnia? What are the essential steps conducive to good sleep?

First let us stress the fact that the major contributing factors in insomnia are habits of overtense living. The individual who has difficulty in falling asleep is overtense during the day and does not work in a relaxed state. Upon retiring and lying down, he endeavors to find a comfortable position in order to sleep, instead of relaxing immediately, even in the presence of minor discomfort.

The primary cause of insomnia is the presence of residual tension. This is the tension left after one lies down but fails to relax completely. Relaxing residual tension sufficiently, and maintaining the relaxed state, brings about sleep and is responsible for the quality of healthful rest and its recuperative powers.

In other words, *Progressive Relaxation is the solution to the problem of insomnia.* The muscles which are to be relaxed in order to induce sleep—in addition to the skeletal muscles—are those of the eyes, and those comprising the speech apparatus. The reason the eyes and speech muscles are so important in this physiological process is that they are among the last to become relaxed. If one starts to relax them first, the other muscles throughout the body relax automatically to a certain extent at the same time. In this sense, they assume the distinction of being "key muscles." *If both the eye and speech muscles are*

Tension, Relaxation, and Related Phenomena

completely relaxed for approximately one-half minute, sleep sets in.

When one desires to sleep at night, but fails, due to an overactive mind, he should cultivate relaxation of all the external body muscles. Then the eye muscles and speech muscles should be relaxed completely, even if for brief periods. Then sleep will come. The quality of sleep will be sound and uninterrupted, so long as the muscles do not become overly tense. The mind also will be at rest.

SCIENTIFIC RELAXATION VS. RELAXATION EXERCISES

Some writers claim that "relaxation exercises" enable a person to attain a relaxed state. Are such claims authentic?

Therapeutic relaxation cannot be attained through "relaxation exercises" as often recommended in various books for worried and nervous persons, some written by members of the healing professions, others by laymen. Let us emphatically state here that *exercises will not teach a person to relax.*

During the training period in progressive relaxation, the performance of tensions is not intended as exercise—but only as a way of learning to perceive when and where one is overtense. This perception enables a person to recognize tension in a part, and adequately prepares him to relax the tension.

Contractions such as stiffening the arms and legs, tensing the abdomen, moving the eyes in different directions, etc., are not performed as an exercise to induce a state of relaxation in that group. There is no objection if exercise is employed toward developing muscle or toward promoting circulation; but contracting muscles—as often recommended—to attain relaxation will not tend to achieve the desired goal.

Our aim is to have you contract a part in order to show you what *not* to do, if you are really to relax there. Laboratory tests have not disclosed the possibility that efficiency in relaxation can be cultivated directly through any form of exercises whatsoever. It has been found that tension of any particular muscle group is not characteristically followed by enduring or progressive relaxation in that group or anywhere else. Besides, if exercises actually were able to bring about advanced states of relaxation, we should expect athletes, physical education instructors, and coaches of various sports to be highly skillful in this art. On the contrary, when examined with laboratory instruments, this group, like other untrained individuals, failed in an extreme degree, to relax and to control their muscular states until they received the necessary training in scientific relaxation. However, they do differ from other individuals in having the tendency to learn faster.

Caution must be used before exercise is recommended as a form of relaxation therapy to nervous persons. Exercise in nervous individuals frequently tends to aggravate their symptoms. By contrast, scientific relaxation, if carried far enough, invariably lessens these symptoms, at least as long as the relaxed state continues. Clinical experience and research discloses that relaxation exercises fall short of serving the purpose to quiet the emotions, reduce nervous irritability and excitement.

There are many authors on relaxation who advocate "relaxation exercises" as a therapeutic measure to eliminate tension and bring about "peace of mind." Their methods are alleged to be scientific, although they never received physiological testing and validation. Surely, any technique proposed to train a person to relax should first be examined by critical scientific measures. Educators in the field of relaxation have a tremendous responsibility to the public. The science is complex and vast, requiring intensive study and preparation. This is too serious a matter to be involved in without the necessary education.

We must stress that from a physiological standpoint there is no reason to expect that various forms of exercise will pro-

Tension, Relaxation, and Related Phenomena

mote the ability to relax to a marked degree under conditions of stress. As is well known, scientific relaxation brings about the elimination of residual tension. It has been found upon careful investigation that after any exercise, relaxation does not as a rule proceed to the point where residual tension vanishes, and it is this which is essential for best results in eliminating nervous and undesirable emotional states.

SOME DATA ABOUT THE MUSCLES

How much of the body weight is composed of muscles?
Muscles compose about half of the weight of the entire body.

How many muscles are there in the human body?
There are eight hundred and forty muscles in the human body.

5
A New Concept of Man in Action

"What must I do to stop worrying?" is a question which victims of this pernicious habit are prone to ask. And the answer is astonishingly simple! In order to stop worrying, you need not do anything with your mind, nor make a conscious effort of any kind—you need only learn to relax your muscles. When the muscles which are directly involved in the process of worrying are properly relaxed, this unhappy state of mind can vanish in as little as one-fifth of a second!

This approach to the problem of attaining and maintaining mental health obviously deviates sharply from the traditional patterns of mental hygiene therapies, entailing as it does a novel concept of man in action. To recognize and accept this new concept—that man "thinks with his muscles" and can therefore control his mental processes through adequate muscular control—will necessarily lead to the modification or discarding of vague, misty theories which have long been accepted as valid in this sphere.

To substantiate this new view of man in action we have ample laboratory and clinical findings. Evidence from both sources indicates that man's actions are subject to controls which to some extent he operates through instinct and without awareness. So that he can recognize these controls consciously and employ them for his benefit in his daily life, he must receive technical training to observe the processes of his own

A New Concept of Man In Action

sensations when confronted with problems in daily living and making environmental adjustments. Evidence also suggests that as a result of this instruction and of habitual application of these controls, he can improve his adaptation to the stresses of present-day living conditions. Besides increasing individual efficiency, the application of such controls will improve social, industrial, and family conduct; it can also be useful internationally, by improving relations between men.

For the reader to gain a clearer understanding of the topic under discussion, we shall liken human beings to very complex machines. While living beings are different in many respects from man-made machines, the controls in man may be compared generally with the driving controls of automobiles which, in operation, determine the rate of speed and the direction of the wheels. Roughly speaking, let us compare the wheels of a motor car with the muscles of a human being, for the muscle fibers, by shortening and lengthening in countless patterns, comprise his endeavors and his actions at every moment of his existence. Numbered among these acts are not only various gross movements of the body, such as walking and running, but also talking, reading, and writing, as well as the operation of his mind, including imagination, recollection and various emotions.

While the brain and other portions of the nervous system participate in every activity of the human organism, they merely carry impulses, like electric wires which conduct messages. However, the brain and nervous system are not capable of the slightest movement.

At the present time the slightest contractions in the muscles of a human being can be electrically measured with scientific exactness (the margin of error is approximately 0.25 millionth of a volt). Direct measurements can now be made of nervous, muscular, or nervous-muscular activity by photographic and pen recordings: in addition an instrument called the integrating neurovoltmeter (developed by Dr. Edmund Jacobson) has made it possible to take measurements of such states even without resort to photography or pen recordings.

Through such highly developed instruments it has become possible to probe into the fundamental problems concerning muscular states and their relations to mental activities, so that formerly prevalent speculation and vague theories concerning the "mind" can now, for the first time in history, be replaced by reality.

In precise studies, it was found that when an individual imagines he is performing an act, he actually performs the act in special muscles, but in a manner so extremely slight and so quickly that the most sensitive instruments are required to detect and register the nerve and muscular actions which, in addition to the brain processes, are engaged.

Now we are certain that brain activity and nervous-muscular activity are concomitant and mutually dependent in the integrated human organism. Mental activities are as dependent upon the muscular system as they are upon the brain, which never acts separately.

Investigations of mental activities with electrophysiology have made it clear why extreme muscular relaxation directly quiets emotional as well as sensory and perceptual states. The person whose electrical measurements from the eye and speech regions measure near zero, is not reflecting at the time. We do not find, as some authors state, that the waking mind is always active or that "it is impossible not to think about something when you are awake."

The direct control of mental operations, like the control of bodily movement, is centered in active muscles. In thought processes or in worrying we turn on an electrical switch, as it were. We can stop worry and the thought processes mechanically by shutting off the switch at will. To worry while relaxation is present is not possible.

We have ample evidence that needless or unmanageable tension of the muscles employed in excessive effort can produce

A New Concept of Man In Action

spasm of the muscles inside the body. Such tension affects the various systems in the body. As one relaxes the skeletal muscles sufficiently (those are the muscles over which one has control), he is relieved of symptoms in the viscera, including the heart, blood vessels (cardiovascular system) and the digestive tract. This comes about because the internal muscles relax. Although not under voluntary control, the organs within the body will relax when the voluntary muscles are relaxed. This shows that excessive tension or spasm in the visceral muscles depends more or less upon the presence of excessive tension in the muscles attached to the skeleton. This being the case, relaxation of skeletal muscles is effective in the treatment of certain internal disorders, since it removes the chief cause of such ailments, or an important part of the cause.

What value will the reader derive from this discussion? The activity of man consists largely of efforts and subefforts, i.e., of major and minor exertions. Effort on the part of the human organism through muscular activity, is analogous to the operation of a machine. The duration of any machine depends upon the care taken of it. Similarly, by knowing where the instrument controls are and utilizing them properly, you can learn to live more intelligently and more efficiently, thus prolonging your span of life. In spite of the fact that the human body has amazing powers of tissue repair and restoration, excessive effort tends in the course of time toward organic disruption and hastens the aging process. You can avoid this useless wear and tear in your body through relaxation.

In millions of persons untrained in the technique of relaxation as a result of the strain of modern living conditions, unawareness of these controls often results in nervous-muscular hypertension. This is partly responsible for most of the common forms of disorders, namely the maladies of self-activation, including anxiety states, insomnia and nervousness. Frequently, this same deficiency in knowledge is conducive to the more serious ailments, including various neurotic conditions, nervous breakdowns, ulcers and spastic colitis, common forms of high blood pressure and even of coronary heart disease.

Drugs, diets, psychotherapy, surgery, and abandoning or fleeing from the irritating environment constitute symptomatic or palliative treatment for these widespread forms of the modern plague besetting humanity. However, they are powerless to strike at the basic cause.

Enough has been said to illustrate and establish the relation of the muscles to the thinking and worrying process. Let us close this chapter with a brief discussion of the mental hygiene subject. Today mental hygiene is not only a national but an international problem. Governmental authorities and educators must realize that a vital step in preventing nervous and mental disorders is the early and adequate education of children. Therefore the schools must play an important role in dealing with this problem. Those who guide the emotional development of children must themselves be emotionally stable. Such education should also be carried out in the home. Parents must take into account that their own stability and the child's home environment will to a great degree determine the emotional health of the child and his behavior pattern as an adult. The medical profession has a towering project of preventive medicine facing it; namely, to teach the populations physiological self-control. But no matter how complex the program may be, this technical knowledge must be conveyed to the masses if we are to solve the problems mentioned above in our own country and in the world at large.

6
The Aim of Scientific Relaxation

Persons reading this volume, whether they are chronic worriers or not, will no doubt ask and expect to receive a logical answer to certain questions. Admittedly, relaxation of muscles will mitigate various tension symptoms or prevent their occurrence. However, how is one to eliminate worry and mental strain in this world of ours if the cause of the stress is not removed?

Coming from an individual who views life on this globe through rose-colored glasses such an argument is not surprising. What an ideal world this would be to live in if the cause of our worries could be removed and all our aspirations for happiness were fulfilled! But the destiny of man precludes such a happy consummation. One must realize that during a lifetime on this earth one may be confronted with illness, physical pain, physical handicaps, economic depressions, accidents, cruelty, selfishness, injustice, stupidity, war, hunger, prejudice, defeat, pestilence, adversity and death.

Since we live in this imperfect world, what is the solution for dealing with the problem of worry? Some will recommend adopting a sound "philosophy of life" as a solution. The question is, does a philosophy of living provide the answer to this problem.

In some people worries can be diminished if they change their outlook on life. Books on popular philosophy are often recommended to patients by their counselors.

We must take into account that philosophies of living vary with individuals and with the era they live in. Observation discloses that when persons learn to relax their muscles, they frequently manifest a philosophy of serenity. So far as we can judge, muscular relaxation precedes the development of this "philosophy" and accounts for its inception.

Persons trained to relax report that as they learn to relax, their reasoning faculty improves. Prehistoric man no doubt tensed and relaxed his many muscles long before he achieved the power of reasoning. He also contracted and relaxed his musculature for ages before he even created a language. When we change habits of tension and relaxation, we are dealing with something more essential, more fundamental than philosophies of living. Persons who are inclined to be worried, fearful or excited behave quite differently when they are calm. Their views then reflect a philosophy of calmness. It is doubtful that a philosophy will in itself radically change habits of restlessness. If a philosophy directly or indirectly should produce a calmer attitude, the end results are physiological; namely, the lengthening and limpness of muscle fibers.

What about methods of inspiration, argument, reassurance and "talking it out" to relieve oneself of worry? It is doubtful whether such measures are sufficiently effective.

The old methods of self-control include one variety which differs from relaxation because it is the very opposite. Every normal person frequently avails himself of it.

"I will control myself," "I will try to forget that unfortunate incident," "I'll snap out of it," you say with determination. Our manner of speaking often manifests itself by what we do with our muscles, and this response of the musculature we inherited from our primitive ancestors. When you express yourself "firmly," just what is it that is firm? Your jaw muscles, and various other muscles throughout your body. You say, "My mind is made up," and often, at that moment, you are tensing your muscles—holding them rigid. This common form of self-

The Aim of Scientific Relaxation

restraint (holding rigid) one learns in his early years from parents and teachers.

We have evidence that this type of behavior is detrimental to our organism. These strains and stresses take a heavy toll in terms of nervous energies, since they involve muscle tension. Holding muscles rigid, even slightly, consumes energy, and in some persons, if it is continuous, it results in strain in various organs.

Cultivated relaxation is far superior because it entails practically no energy output. Even if long continued, this type of control is not followed by exhaustion or any other harmful effect, and it succeeds in bringing about a marked reduction in one's habits of worrying and grieving.

What attitude should a person assume when catastrophes occur? Individuals surely cannot be indifferent to the misfortunes of life—indeed not! If serious illness strikes you or members of your family, if financial disaster comes, if death takes some relative or friend—these are misfortunes which no method of relaxation intends to teach you to confront with cheerfulness. Where such teachings do occur, they are associated with certain religious and ascetic beliefs; they instill an apathy or an indifference to fate. Adherence to such esoteric philosophies produces an unnatural way of life in man.

An emotionally stable person should grieve when tragedy strikes, should worry at times that things may not turn out well. But worrying and grieving should have sensible limits. They should be controlled when they threaten to destroy health and happiness, when they impair efficiency for a lengthy period. The scientific aspects of this control, in the form of cultivated relaxation, constitute the essence of this thesis.

Through training in scientific relaxation the individual acquires the ability to observe his own muscular sensations when he faces daily problems and makes adjustments to environment. When faced with troubling situations he has the ability to *distinguish between the issue and tension-attitude.*

Let us be realistic—no human being can be so fortunate as to live a lifetime without some tribulations. Surmounting adversity or obstacles to existence comes in learning to absorb the shocks or knowing "how to take it." To repeat; through real relaxation we achieve flexibility of body and mind. Therefore, whatever the blows that life has in store for us, we are ready to accept them since we have the technique, equipment, strength and inner peace to make the necessary adjustments.

This then is the blessing of scientific relaxation, which most people can learn and apply in their living. Where is there a greater and simpler benefit awaiting a worried humanity, still largely unaware of these possibilities and searching for relief almost entirely in the increasing use of sedative drugs? It is very doubtful if medications will ever bring to a person the ideal state of peace of mind. We know that studied relaxation processes can bring about this tranquility.

7
Technique of General Relaxation

THE TECHNIQUE of scientific relaxation is presented here in a series of steps which require practice. It is important that you complete the entire course of instruction. A practice period should consist of at least forty-five minutes or one hour in seclusion. Make certain you are not disturbed. You may devote one or two periods a day to practice, if possible, setting aside the same times each day for this purpose.

Select a quiet room which contains a bed or couch. A thin pillow is recommended to support the head. The room does not necessarily have to be dark. "General relaxation" training involves relaxing flat on your back. However, when you go to sleep or take a nap, assume any position to which you are accustomed.

During practice, do not fold your hands or cross the legs. Each arm in its entire length should rest several inches from the sides of the body.

Also during practice, whenever the instructions specify that the eyes be closed, you should remember not to shut the eyes quickly or abruptly, but, instead, gradually close the eyelids lightly, permitting about three minutes to elapse before you shut them completely. Then you are to keep your eyes closed for the entire practice session. This is effective in bringing about a more gradual letdown.

At this point it is also necessary to clarify the time element in practice periods. You will be instructed to allot a certain specified time to the various aspects of the technique. Since watching a timepiece interferes with the process of relaxation, exact timing is not essential—you need only concern yourself with an estimate of the timing to the best of your ability, and you will still obtain the desired results.

In the course of training, every third practice period should be devoted to *complete relaxation only*. This session, devoted entirely to repose, is called a "zero period." For example, perform no tensions in practice periods numbered three, six, nine, twelve, fifteen and subsequent multiples of three.

Before proceeding with the technique of relaxation, we wish to emphasize that at *no* time during the training period or thereafter, should you try to induce relaxation by talking to yourself—or to your muscles. *Never* repeat such phrases as, "I am relaxing," or, "I am going limp," or "Let go, let go," or "This will do me good," etc. Auto-suggestion is actually a hindrance in learning to relax.

Please remember this very important factor. Only during the training period, when the technique is being learned, do you purposely tense the various muscles of your body prior to relaxation. *The contraction (tension) is performed so that you may acquire the skill to recognize the sensation of tension* in its varying degrees. When you are *not* practicing, *do not tense* in order to relax. Except for the purpose of reviewing the technique in some parts of your body after you have completed the course of instruction, *do not perform any preliminary tensing in order to relax*. Proficiency in recognizing the feeling of tension in any part of the body, and relaxing such tension will in time, through practice and application, result in an automatic "let go"; it will maintain that state with little or no active attention. Relaxation then becomes second nature to you.

In the illustrations referring to the technique, the location of the sensation of tenseness in various parts of the body, will be designated by the white areas.

Technique of General Relaxation

We shall now proceed with the presentation of the various steps of the technique in the lying down position.

STEP I: RELAXING THE ARMS
Practice—three periods

Lie flat on your back. Place your arms at your sides, palms down, several inches from the body, legs at full length (Fig. 1). Relax to the best of your present ability. Make sure that you are allowing the bed to receive your full weight. After taking about three minutes to close the eyes gradually and lightly, keep them closed throughout the entire practice period.

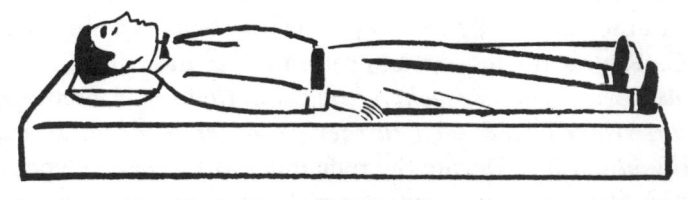

Figure 1

A. After approximately ten minutes of such relaxation—without moving your arms—slowly stiffen the muscles slightly in both arms in their entirety, without clenching your fists. Hold it at this degree of stiffness for about ten seconds. Now stiffen a little more and hold still—a little more and hold. Maintain that rigidity in the arms for about thirty seconds. Carefully observe a distinct feeling throughout both arms. *This sensation is the experience of tension.* It occurs when a muscle contracts. This feeling, called the "tension-sense," is a signal of nervous-muscular activity. It is under your voluntary control, and may also be termed the "control sensation." You *must* become familiar with this feeling of tenseness—no matter where it occurs in the body or how slight it may be—so that you can rid yourself of it! As you become aware of the sensation of tenseness in your arms, realize that *you* alone are responsible for its presence because *you are doing something!* This "doing" involves *effort* on your part. What we want is the opposite of effort—that is, simply, "not doing"!

Now, slowly, let go, slightly, of the stiffness in both arms and hold it. Let go a little more and hold; still a little more—a little more—observing as you do that the feeling in the arms diminishes in intensity. *Now let go completely,* and note that the sensation in the arms disappears. The disappearance or absence of this sensation is *relaxation.* This illustrates progressive tension and relaxation in the arm muscles.

Maintain such relaxation for about five minutes.

B. Repeat the tension and relaxation as in *A,* and make your observation. Relax completely for about five minutes.

C. Repeat the tension and relaxation as in *A* and *B. Then relax beyond the stage where you think that the arms are perfectly relaxed, and even further, in order to do away with residual tension.* Devote the remainder of the practice period to *complete relaxation,* without performing any more tensions. *You must not resume tensing the muscles from time to time, or you will destroy the benefits derived from this relaxation.*

Bear in mind that *true relaxation involves no effort,* while tension does. You did not have to do anything in order to relax! However, you did have to put forth effort, or *do* something, in order to tense your muscles. During tense states, muscle fibers contract, producing the sensation or experience called the "tension-sense," while during a completely relaxed state muscles are limp. Do not make the mistake of contracting or tensing various muscles in *an effort* to relax. Tensing to relax is called the "effort error." Do not make difficult what should be perfectly natural.

Technique of General Relaxation

Remember: 1) When you are performing tensions to discern the tension-sense, you are *not exercising,* for no exercise will teach you to relax. The tensions will help you to perceive the sensation of tenseness, so that you will know where you are overtense in various parts of your body. This will enable you to relax those regions.
2) Do not tense to relax: should this occur, let go at once.
3) Make no effort to relax. You will find that making such effort is being tense—and therefore is not relaxation.
4) The feeling of tenseness in your skeletal muscles is under your voluntary control. Concern yourself in becoming familiar with this "control sensation" in every part of your body, so that you can learn to manage yourself, properly relaxed, under all circumstances.
5) Every third practice period should be devoted only to complete relaxation. Do not perform any tensions. However, if you should do so, consciously or unconsciously, observe the slight "control sensation" and relax in that region at once.
6) Abstain from moving during relaxation: however do not "hold yourself still." "Holding still" means that you are tensing, by faint continuous contraction of muscles. This is not true relaxation but merely a useless imitation.
7) Complete relaxation means doing away with residual tension. Note how this sensation of tenseness is overlooked because of its faint-

ness, unless brought to your attention. Be patient—with practice you will acquire the necessary skill.

STEP II: RELAXING THE LEGS
Practice—three periods

A. Lie on your back as previously instructed. After ten minutes of complete relaxation, stiffen the muscles in both legs in their entirety without moving them. Begin by making the muscles a little rigid, a little more—a little more—gradually increasing the stiffness until the maximum is reached. Hold the legs in this rigid state for about fifteen seconds. Note the extraordinary sensation of tenseness throughout both legs. This feeling is present in your legs because *you are* doing something! Now let go a little of the tension and hold it. Let go a little more and hold. Continue letting go—or "going negative," as this is called—a little at a time, observing that the sensation diminishes in intensity as you do so. Then let go entirely and note that the tension in both legs disappears. The absence of the feeling of tension is *relaxation*. Maintain this relaxation for about five minutes.

B. Repeat the tension and relaxation as in *A*, and make your observation. Relax completely for about five minutes.

C. Repeat *B*. Relax completely for remainder of practice period.

Remember: While learning to relax the legs, make sure not to perform any tensions in the arms. Keep the arms completely relaxed during the entire practice session.

STEP III: RELAXING THE TRUNK AND NECK
1. Relaxing the Chest
Practice—two periods

A. Lie on your back as previously instructed. Following fifteen minutes of complete relaxation, breathe a little more

Technique of General Relaxation

deeply than usual and hold your breath for about five seconds (Fig. 2). Now breathe out. Note the tension in the chest while you inhale, and the relaxation as you exhale. Let the chest go, just as you did with the arms and legs, permitting the breathing to take its natural course. Relax for about five minutes.

B. Repeat the tension in *A*. Again observe tension during a deeper breath. Let the chest go and relax for the remainder of period.

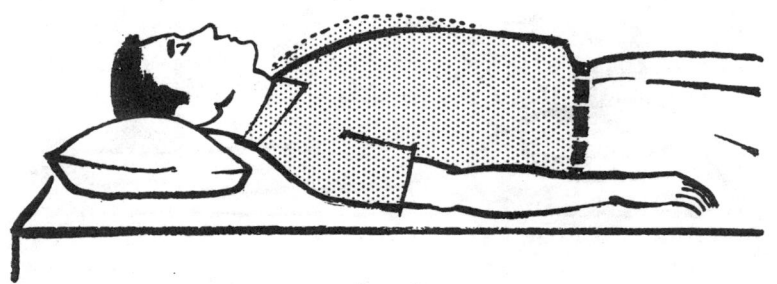

Figure 2

Remember: 1) While relaxing the chest, make sure not to perform any tensions in the arms and legs, which are to be completely relaxed during the entire practice session.
2) Do not use "controlled breathing" as an aid in relaxation. Respiration should be free from voluntary influence.

2. RELAXING THE ABDOMEN AND BACK
Practice—two periods

A. Lie on your back as previously instructed. After ten minutes of relaxation, draw in the abdominal muscles for fifteen seconds (Fig. 3). Note the sensation of tension over the entire front of the abdomen. Let the abdomen go and relax for about five minutes.

B. Repeat the tension in *A*. Relax for about five minutes.

C. Arch the back for about fifteen seconds (Fig. 4). Note the tension along both sides of the spine. Let the back go and relax for about five minutes.

D. Repeat *C*. Relax completely for remainder of period.

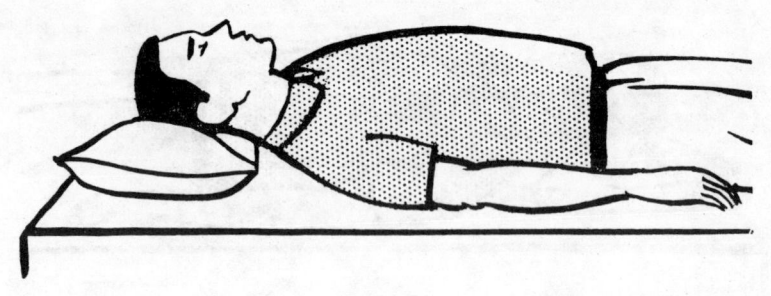

Figure 3

Remember: Keep arms, legs and chest completely relaxed while learning to relax the abdomen and back.

3. RELAXING THE SHOULDERS AND NECK
Practice—two periods

A. Assume position as previously instructed. Following ten minutes of relaxation, stiffen the shoulder muscles slightly. Stiffen them a little more and hold at that degree—a little more—and maintain that rigidity for about thirty seconds. Note the marked sensation of tenseness throughout the shoulder muscles. Now let the shoulders go a little and hold—a little more

Technique of General Relaxation

and hold. Now let go completely, observing the disappearance of the tension in the shoulders. Relax for about five minutes.

B. Repeat the tension in *A*. Relax for about five minutes.

C. Slightly stiffen the muscles of the entire neck. Stiffen them a little more—a little more. Hold the muscles in this rigid

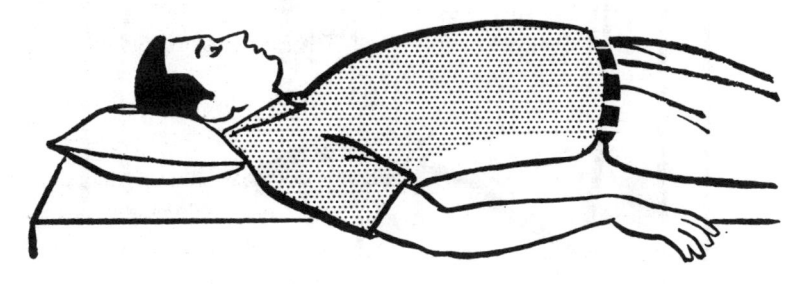

Figure 4

state for about fifteen seconds. Note the extraordinary feeling of tenseness in the entire neck. Now let the muscles relax slightly and hold at that degree. Let go a little more and hold it. Continue letting go—a little more—then let go completely, until the tension in the neck muscles disappears. Relax for about five minutes.

D. Repeat *C*. Relax for remainder of period.

Remember: While relaxing the shoulders and neck, make sure you are completely relaxed in the regions which had previous practice.

STEP IV: RELAXING THE EYE REGIONS AND EYES

1. RELAXING THE FOREHEAD, BROW AND EYELIDS
Practice—three periods

A. Assume position as previously instructed. Following ten

minutes of relaxation, wrinkle the forehead upward for about one minute (Fig. 5). Note the tension beneath the wrinkling

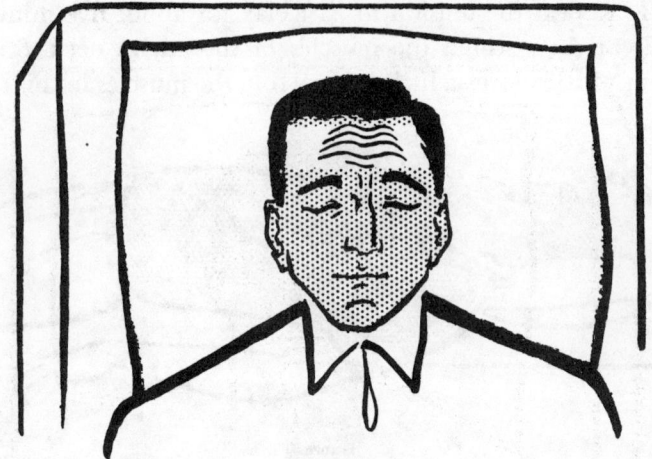

Figure 5

skin of the entire forehead. Let the forehead go and relax for about five minutes.

B. Frown deeply for about one minute. Observe the tension

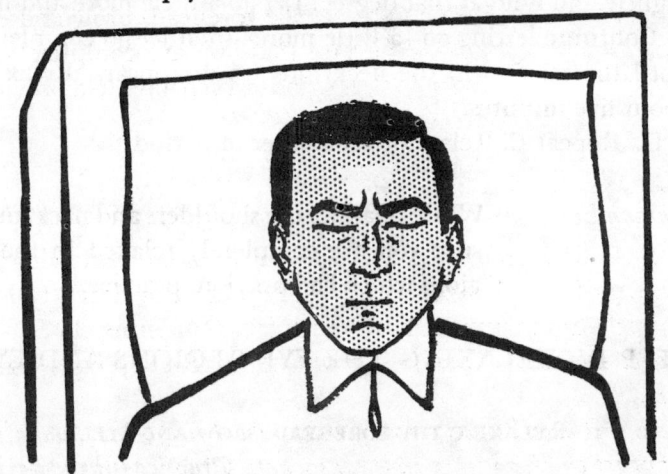

Figure 6

in the region between the eyes (Fig. 6). Let the frown go and relax for about five minutes.

Technique of General Relaxation

C. Close eyelids tightly for about one minute. Note the tension in the lids (Fig. 7). Let the lids go and relax for remainder of period.

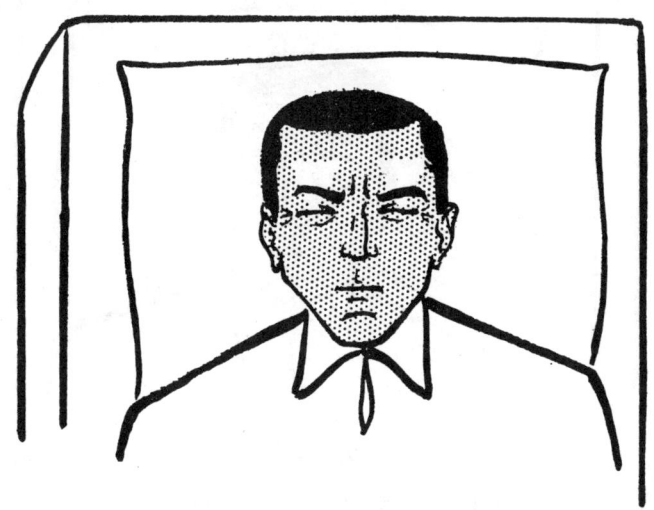

Figure 7

Remember: While relaxing the forehead, brow and eyelids, make sure that you are completely relaxed in the regions which have had previous practice.

2. RELAXING THE EYES
Practice—three periods

A. Assume position as previously instructed. Following ten minutes of complete relaxation with eyelids closed lightly, look up, without moving the head (with eyes remaining closed) for fifteen seconds. Note the tenseness in the eyeball region (Fig. 8).

Now relax the eyes completely. *To bring this relaxation about let them go limp in their sockets.* Observe that when the eyes are completely relaxed they simply are *not looking* in any direction. Relax completely for about five minutes.

B. Again look up for fifteen seconds. Note the tension in

eyeball region. Let the eyes go completely as directed in *A*, and relax for about five minutes.

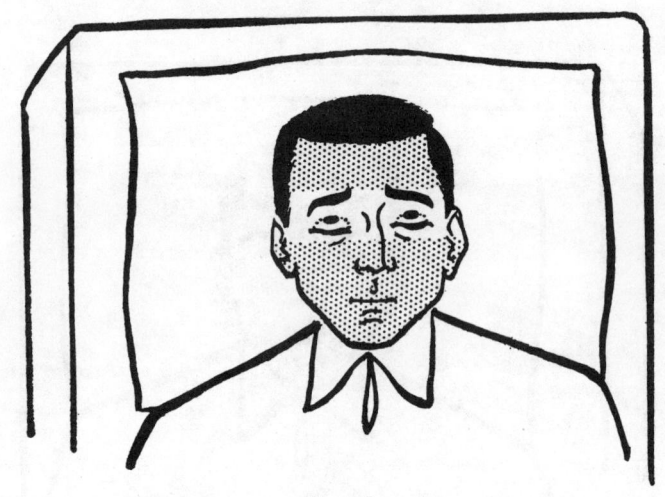

Figure 8

C. Look down for fifteen seconds. Note the tension in the eyeball region (Fig. 9). Let the eyes go completely, and relax for about five minutes.

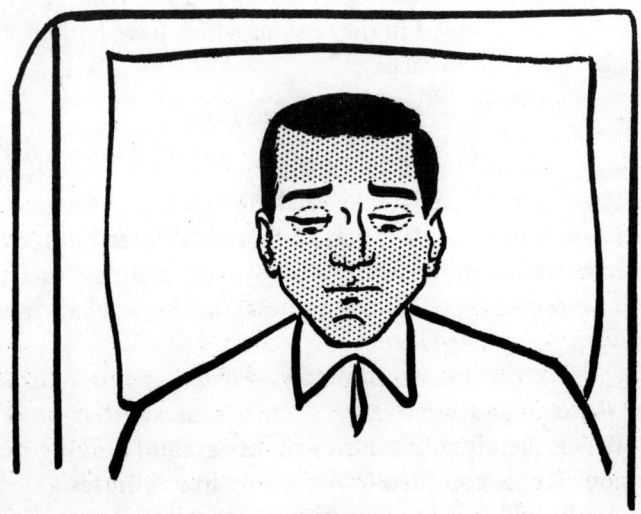

Figure 9

Technique of General Relaxation

D. Repeat *C*. Relax for remainder of period.

3
Practice—three periods

A. Assume position as previously instructed. Following ten minutes of relaxation, look to the left (without moving the head) for fifteen seconds (Fig. 10). Note the tension in the eyeball region. Let the eyes go completely, and relax for about five minutes.

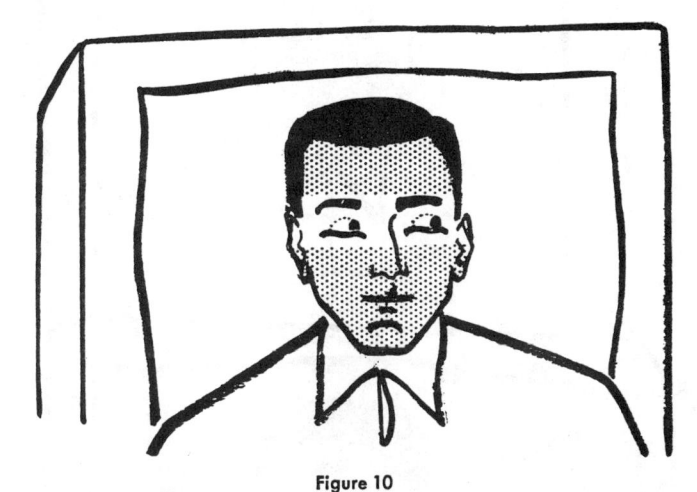

Figure 10

B. Look to the right for fifteen seconds (Fig. 11). Note tension in eyeball region. Let the eyes go completely, and relax for about five minutes.

C. Look straight forward for about one minute (Fig. 12). Note the static tension in the eyeball region. Let the eyes go completely and relax for the remainder of practice period.

Remember: 1) The ability to relax the eyes, including the brow and lids, requires considerable skill.
2) Let the eyes go in the same manner as you relaxed the arms, legs, and other parts of the body that have received practice.

3) When relaxing the eyes, *let them go so that they are simply not looking. Permit them to become limp in their sockets.*

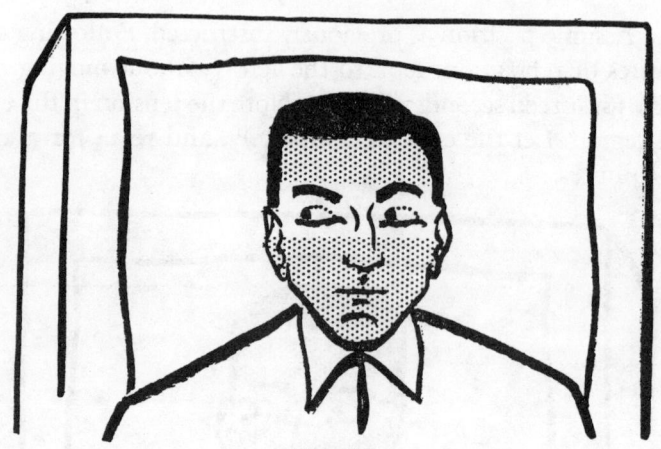

Figure 11

Figure 12

4) If you have difficulty in relaxing the eyeballs, stiffen the right arm slightly, then gradually let your *arm and eyes relax together.*

Technique of General Relaxation

5) While relaxing the eyeballs, let go the arms, legs, abdomen, chest, back, shoulders, neck, forehead, brow and eyelids.

STEP V: RELAXING MENTAL ACTIVITIES

1. VISUAL IMAGERY
Practice—three periods

A. Lie on your back with eyes closed. Following ten minutes of complete relaxation, *imagine* yourself walking slowly from left to right. Note the instant visual picture of yourself accompanied by a slight feeling of tenseness in the eyeballs, as if the eyes are moving from left to right.

Now relax the eyes completely. In so doing, observe that the picture or visual image in your eyes disappears. Relax completely for about ten minutes.

B. Imagine yourself walking rapidly from right to left. Again note a flashlike visual image of yourself accompanied by a slight sensation of tenseness in the eyeballs, as if the eyes are following your motions.

Let the eyes go completely. Upon such relaxation, note that the visual image in your eyes disappears. Relax for remainder of period.

2
Practice—three periods

A. Assume position as previously instructed. Following ten minutes of complete relaxation, imagine yourself climbing a flight of steps. Note the instant visual picture of yourself followed by a slight feeling of tenseness in the eyeballs, as if the eyes are moving upward following you.

Now relax the eyes completely. In doing so observe the disappearance of the visual picture in your eyes. Relax for about five minutes.

B. Imagine yourself descending the flight of steps. Again

note the visual picture of yourself, accompanied by the slight tension in the eyeballs, as they move downward following your descent.

Relax the eyes completely, observing the disappearance of the visual image in your eyes. Relax for about five minutes.

C. Imagine several horses running around a race track, and make similar observation. Relax for about five minutes.

D. Imagine a picture of the President of the United States. Note that you experience the same kind of tenseness in the eyeballs as occurred when you imagined a moving object, ex-

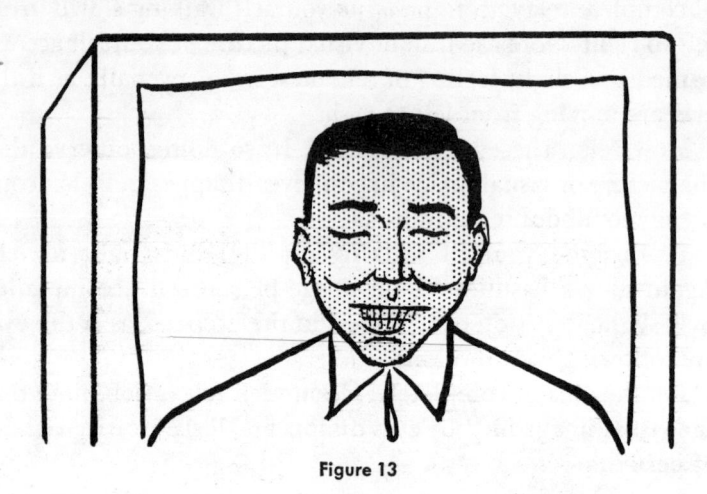

Figure 13

cept now the tension is steady as you look at a fixed object. Let the eyes go completely. Upon such relaxation note that the visual image in your eyes disappears. Relax for remainder of period.

Remember: 1) Let the eyes go so that they become limp in their sockets.

2) When you relax the eyes completely, thereby doing away with the minute tensions that occur during imagination, you will find that

Technique of General Relaxation

the mind ceases to be active. In this way you obtain a desired form of mental control.

3) While relaxing visual imagery, make sure that you are not performing any tensions in the parts of the body that have received previous practice.

STEP VI: RELAXING THE SPEECH REGION

1. RELAXING THE JAWS, CHEEKS AND LIPS
Practice—two periods

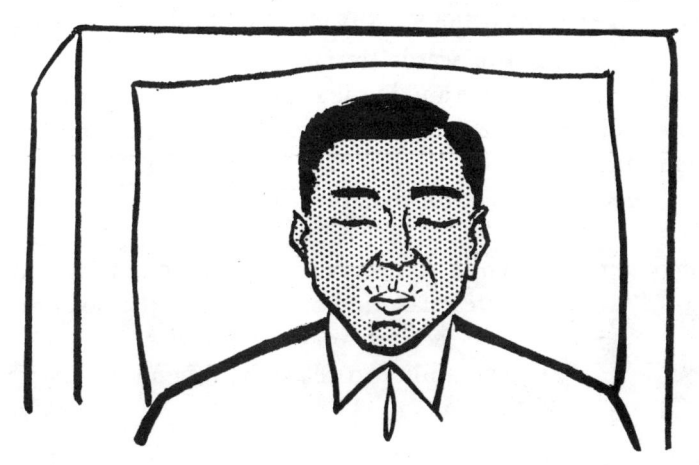

Figure 14

A. Assume position as previously instructed. Following ten minutes of relaxation, close jaws firmly for thirty seconds. Note the tension extending from the angle of the jaws up to the temples. Let the jaws go and relax for about five minutes.

B. Open jaws for thirty seconds. Observe tension in front of ears. Let the jaws go and relax for about five minutes.

C. Smile, showing your teeth, for thirty seconds (Fig. 13). Note tension in the cheeks. Let the cheeks go and relax for about five minutes.

D. Round your lips in a pout for thirty seconds. Note tension in the lips (Fig. 14). Let the lips go and relax for remainder of period.

2. RELAXING THE TONGUE
Practice—two periods

A. Assume position as previously instructed. Following ten minutes of relaxation, press tongue forward against front teeth for thirty seconds. Observe tenseness in the tongue. Let the tongue go and relax for about five minutes.

B. Repeat the tension in *A*. Relax for about five minutes.

C. Pull tongue backwards (retract) for thirty seconds. Note tenseness in the tongue and in the region behind the chin, and the floor of the mouth. Let the tongue go and relax for about five minutes.

D. Repeat *C*. Relax for remainder of period.

Remember: 1) While you relax the tongue, maintain complete relaxation of all parts of the body that have received previous practice.
2) The ability to relax the tongue is very important.

STEP VII: RELAXING THE SPEECH APPARATUS

1

Practice—two periods

A. Assume position as previously instructed. Following fifteen minutes of complete relaxation, slowly recite aloud the alphabet from A to G. As you produce each sound, carefully note the tension in your tongue, lips, jaw regions, throat, diaphragm and all over the chest. Relax all parts mentioned, and observe that the sensation of tenseness disappears in these regions. Maintain such relaxation for about five minutes.

Technique of General Relaxation

B. Again slowly recite the alphabet from A to G, this time half as loud as in *A*. Carefully observe that the same tensions are present in the same regions described in *A*, but are less intense in character. Let go all parts, and relax for about five minutes.

C. Slowly recite the alphabet from A to G in a whisper. Note the presence of slight tenseness in the same regions described in *A* and *B*. Let go all parts and completely relax for remainder of period.

2

Practice—two periods

A. Assume position as previously instructed. After fifteen minutes of relaxation, slowly recite the alphabet from A to G, in such manner that one cannot see the motion of your lips or hear you make a sound. Carefully observe the slight tension in the speech apparatus. Relax for about five minutes.

B. *Imagine* that you are slowly reciting the alphabet from A to G. Note the *very slight* sensation of tension in the parts comprising the speech apparatus. Let the speech apparatus go completely, relaxing the muscles of the tongue, lips, jaw regions, throat, diaphragm and chest. Bear in mind that during *imagination* and when you are actually reciting aloud or half as loud—or whispering, or reciting imperceptibly—the sensation of tenseness in the speech apparatus is the same except for varying degrees of intensity. Maintain such relaxation for about five minutes.

C. Repeat tension in *B*.

D. Repeat C. Relax for remainder of period.

Remember: 1) Note that when you completely relax the speech apparatus you no longer "speak" to yourself.
2) Skill is required to relax the speech apparatus. Practice to gain that proficiency.
3) While you are learning to relax the speech appartus, maintain complete relaxation of

all parts of the body that have received previous practice.

STEP VIII: RELAXING THE MIND
Practice—six periods

A. Assume position as previously instructed. Make sure that your entire body, eyes and the speech apparatus are completely relaxed. After ten minutes of such relaxation, *imagine* that you are discussing the weather with a friend at your home. Observe very closely what is now taking place—the instant you begin to think of this, you get a mental "picture" along with a slight tension in the eye muscles, as you see your friend, yourself, and the surroundings where the conversation takes place. At the same instant, carefully note the slight tension which appears in your speech apparatus.

The "pictures" you see in the process of thinking or in imagination are called visual images; the activity (tension) in your vocal apparatus is termed "inner speech."

What you have observed should make it clear to you that mental activity includes brain plus muscle action in an inseparable combination.

Now completely relax the eyes and the speech mechanism. Carefully note that when you do so, the "pictures" in your mind disappear and "inner speech" ceases. *You have stopped thinking! Now you have reached the desired stage of mental control.*

Maintain such relaxation for about ten minutes.

B. *Imagine* conversing with someone on the telephone. Again note the slight tension in your eyes and speech apparatus as you visualize, and talk to yourself through inner speech, during this procedure. Let the muscles in these regions go and observe how the visual imagery disappears and inner speech ceases. Relax completely for remainder of period.

Remember: In an effort to stop thinking you are at *no time* to *try* to make your mind a "blank."

Technique of General Relaxation

Just relax your muscles and the rest will take care of itself.

STEP IX: RELAXING WORRY

Practice—ten periods

In this step you will be instructed in the technique of relaxing worry (with eyes remaining closed), taking as an example the possibility of losing your position as the needless anxiety or fear. However, you may substitute in its place any worry or particular fear which may be troubling you.

A. Assume position as previously instructed. Make sure that your entire body including the eyes and speech apparatus are completely relaxed. After about fifteen minutes of such relaxation, start "worrying" that you may lose your job. Observe very closely what is now taking place—the instant you begin to worry, you have a mental picture, along with a slight tension in the eye muscles. You are *visualizing* the various unpleasant details and the consequences of losing your position. Note that you are seeing various mental pictures related to the troubling situation. The phenomenon in the eyes can be likened to a motion picture projected on a screen.

Of course you now realize that you are *looking directly* at your worry. At the same instant, carefully observe the very slight tension in your speech apparatus. In addition to *seeing* your worry, you are actually *talking* or representing, *over and over again* to yourself, or to others, the nature of the trouble, without producing a sound! This inner speech is rapid, slurred, and the words are telescoped.

Some persons may not experience marked visual imagery when they worry; others, on the other hand, may experience both visualization and inner speech during the worry process.

This observation should make it clear to you that "worrying" includes brain plus muscle action in an inseparable combination.

Now completely relax the eyes and the speech apparatus.

Again carefully note that when you do so, the mental pictures disappear and inner speech ceases. *For the present you have stopped worrying!*

Let us emphasize at this point that you have stopped worrying because you have relaxed, to an extreme degree, your eyes and speech apparatus, which are the key regions controlling thought (and worry) processes.

Maintain complete relaxation for ten minutes.

Until you become sufficiently skillful in relaxing your worries, you will undoubtedly have some recurrence of undesirable mental pictures and inner speech involved in the process of worry. Observe when this occurs that *you* are *tensing* the eye and speech (key) regions. *Relax these parts whenever the worry makes its appearance.*

B. Again, in imagination, choose to worry about something, and make your observation as in *A*. Let go all the muscles involved in the worry (thinking) process, and relax completely for the remainder of the practice period.

Remember:
1) Make sure when relaxing worry to completely let go the forehead, brow and eyelids, together with the eye and speech regions.
2) You are tensing muscles whenever you worry.
3) In the early stages of practice, relief from worry may not be constant. However, beneficial results in the form of nearly complete relief will be acquired through diligent practice and application of the technique as outlined in this work.
4) The desired goal in relaxing worry is attained when relaxation becomes "second nature," so that the worry process can be "shut off" much like an electric switch, at will and at any time.

8
Technique of Differential Relaxation

THE WORRIER must not only be taught how to relax lying down, but also needs instruction on how to relax during his activities. This is accomplished by his acquiring a new habit of being relaxed while in an upright posture. Progressive relaxation offers a method whereby the active individual can perform his daily activities and carry on his business and social affairs with undiminished efficiency, while at the same time he can replace worry, irritability and excitement with calm nerves.

Relaxation during activity is called "differential relaxation." The most important principle in the application of relaxation during activities may be expressed as follows: *It means using the minimum of tensions in the muscles required for an act, while at the same time other muscles are relaxed.* Differential relaxation is essential in the performances of all duties, if maximum efficiency is to be attained and maintained.

Certain muscular contractions are necessary in the performance of a task. These are called "primary tensions." Certain other tensions are not necessary in the performance of that task; for example, those tensions which arise when a person is distracted or when he reflects about irrelevant matters while so engaged at that duty. Such tensions are termed "secondary." Differential relaxation aids in doing away with secondary tensions, and to reduce primary tensions whenever these are excessive.

The author's book, *How to Free Yourself From Nervous Tension,* covers this subject in greater detail.

Practicing relaxation in the sitting position will help you relax differentially during work or play and at home. You will observe the muscle tensions needed to perform any activity at any time. You will also observe which muscles need not be used and should therefore be relaxed. Furthermore, you may find that you have been using more muscular effort in your work than is necessary—thereby *overexerting* yourself and wasting precious energy, which frequently brings about excessive fatigue and useless wear and tear on the body, especially to the *heart.*

Learn to ease up and see how your efficiency will be improved through an economy of energy.

In learning this new phase of relaxation it is important to remember the following directions: During practice periods, unless instructed otherwise, you are to relax all parts of the body in the sitting position with eyes closed. While sitting, hold the back stiff enough to prevent yourself from falling off the chair, but no more than that.

Select a chair that has arms long enough and sufficiently wide upon which to rest your arms.

Your posture in a sitting position should be as follows (Fig. 15): the arms should rest on and be supported by both arms of the chair; the legs are more or less sprawled out; the head should droop limply, and breathing be regular and quiet. All indications of restlessness are absent. The eyelids do not wink during a prolonged period, and the eyeballs should reveal no motion.

We shall review in the sitting posture a shorter course of relaxation than employed while lying down.

The tensions performed in the sitting posture during prac-

Technique of Differential Relaxation

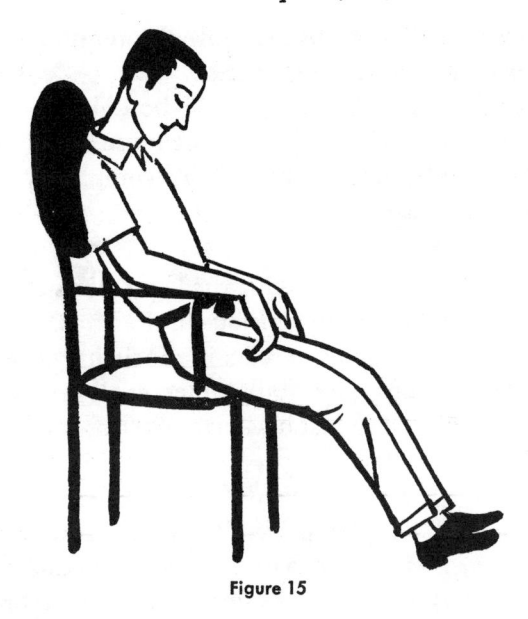

Figure 15

tice are to be relatively slight. The reason for this is to cultivate the experience of the sensation of muscular contraction in its most minute form.

STEP X: RELAXING THE ARMS AND LEGS
Practice—two periods

Sit in an armchair, both arms resting on arm supports, head drooping limply, and legs sprawled out in front of you. The eyes should be kept open for approximately three minutes, then gradually closed lightly, and kept closed throughout the entire practice period.

A. Following ten minutes of relaxation, slightly stiffen the muscles of both arms without clenching the fists, so that they become slightly rigid while resting on arms of chair. Maintain the slight rigidity in the arms for about one minute. Carefully observe the feeling of tenseness throughout both arms. Now let go completely and observe how the tension in the arms fades. Relax for about five minutes.

B. Slightly stiffen the muscles of both legs and hold for about one minute. Carefully note the tension throughout the legs. Let go, relaxing the legs. Relax completely for the remainder of practice period.

Remember: 1) While relaxing the legs make sure not to perform any tensions in the arms.
2) When you relax in the sitting position, make sure that you also let go all the parts of your body that have had practice in a supine position.
3) Relax *beyond* the stage where you think that you are perfectly relaxed, and even further, in order to do away with residual tension.
4) Omit all tensions every third practice period. Just relax completely.

STEP XI: RELAXING THE TRUNK AND NECK

1. RELAXING THE CHEST AND ABDOMEN
Practice—two periods

A. Assume position as previously instructed. Following fifteen minutes of relaxation, with the arms and legs fully relaxed, breathe in deeper than usual. Hold it for five seconds. Now breathe out. Note the tension in the chest while you inhale, and the relaxation as you exhale. Let the chest go, just as you did with the arms and legs, permitting the breathing to take its natural course. Do not use "controlled breathing" as an aid in relaxation. Respiration should be free from voluntary influence. Relax completely for about ten minutes.

B. Pull in abdomen slightly for fifteen seconds. Note ten-

Technique of Differential Relaxation

sion over the entire front of abdomen. Let the abdomen go and relax for remainder of period.

2. RELAXING THE BACK AND SHOULDERS
Practice—two periods

Figure 16

A. Assume position as previously instructed. Following ten minutes of relaxation, sit up straight for one minute (Fig. 16). Observe the tension along both sides of the spine. Let the back go and relax for about five minutes.

B. Slightly stiffen the shoulder muscles for one minute. Note tension in the shoulders. Let the shoulders go and relax for remainder of period.

3. RELAXING THE NECK
Practice—two periods

A. Assume position as previously instructed. After ten minutes of relaxation, slightly stiffen the muscles of the entire neck for one minute. Observe the tension in the neck. Let the neck go and relax for about ten minutes.

B. Repeat the tension in *A*. Relax for remainder of period.

Remember: While relaxing neck make sure that you maintain complete relaxation of all parts of the body that have received previous practice.

STEP XII: RELAXING THE FOREHEAD, BROW AND EYELIDS

Practice—three periods

A. Assume position as previously instructed. After ten minutes of relaxation, slightly wrinkle the forehead upward for

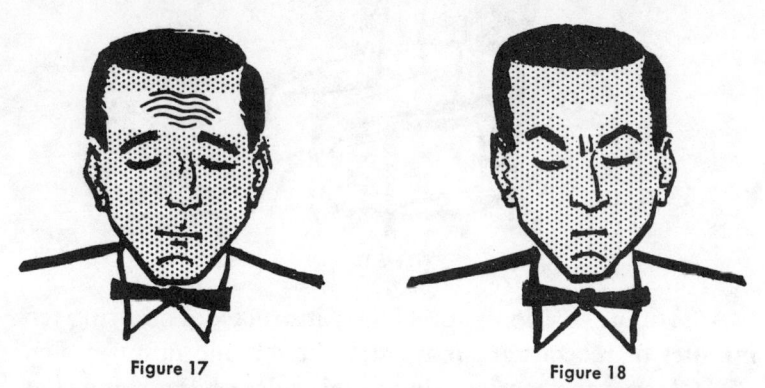

Figure 17

Figure 18

one minute (Fig. 17). Note the tension beneath the wrinkling skin of entire forehead. Let the forehead go, and relax for about five minutes.

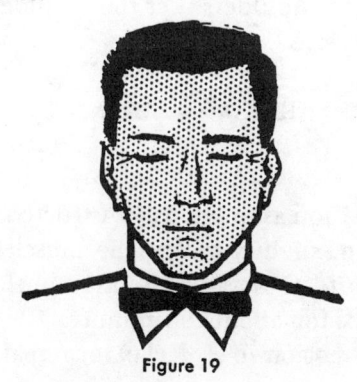

Figure 19

Technique of Differential Relaxation

B. Frown slightly for one minute (Fig. 18). Observe tension in the region between the eyes. Let the frown go and relax for about five minutes.

C. Close eyelids slightly tighter than normally for one minute (Fig. 19). Note tension in lids. Let the lids go and relax for remainder of period.

Remember: While relaxing the forehead, brow, and eyelids, maintain complete relaxation of the arms, legs, abdomen, chest, back, neck and shoulders.

STEP XIII: RELAXING THE EYES
Practice—three periods

A. Sit in a chair with *eyes open,* head erect. Following ten minutes of relaxation in this position, look up for about fifteen seconds without moving the head (Fig. 20). Note the tension in the eyeball region.

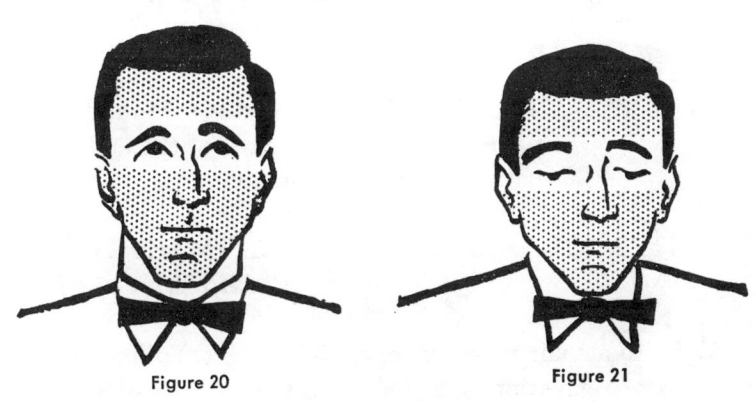

Figure 20

Figure 21

Now relax the eyes completely, letting them go limp in their sockets. *Observe that when the eyes are completely relaxed they simply are not looking in any direction.*

Now look down for fifteen seconds (Fig. 21). Note the tension in the eyeball region. Let the eyes go completely, and relax for about five minutes.

B. Look to the left for fifteen seconds (Fig. 22). Note the tension in the eyeball region. Relax the eyes.

Look to the right for fifteen seconds (Fig. 23). Note the tension in eyeball region. Let the eyes go completely and relax for about five minutes.

C. Look straight forward for one minute (Fig. 24). Note the static tension in the eyeball region. Let the eyes go completely. Relax for remainder of period.

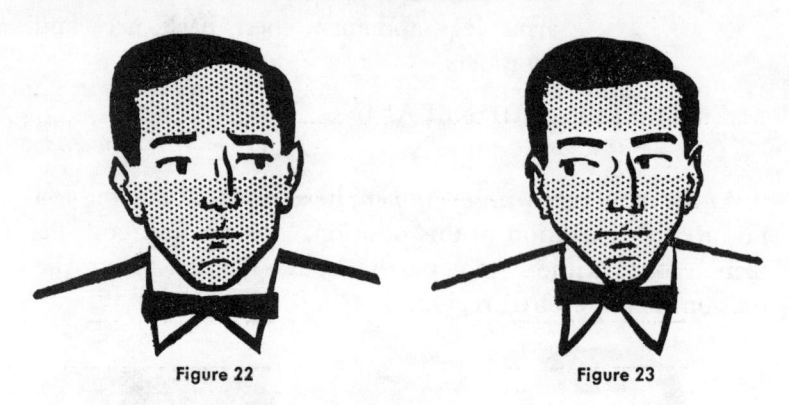

Figure 22

Figure 23

Remember: While relaxing the eyeballs, maintain complete relaxation of all parts of the body that have received previous practice.

STEP XIV: RELAXING VISUAL IMAGERY
Practice—three periods

A. Sit in a chair with *eyes* open, head erect. Following ten minutes of relaxation, imagine an automobile passing from left to right. Observe the tenseness in the eyeballs the instant you visualize the vehicle, as if the eyes are turning to follow the moving car. Carefully note that the feeling of tension in the eyes, although very faint, has the same characteristic sensation that is present in the larger muscles when under contraction.

Relax the eyes completely, ceasing to move the eyes in any

Technique of Differential Relaxation

direction or to look forward, yet not holding them still. Let them become lax in their sockets. Upon relaxing the eyeballs completely, note the disappearance of the visual picture in your eyes. Relax completely for about five minutes.

B. Imagine a train passing quickly from right to left. Your observation should disclose a flashlike visual picture of a train, accompanied by a slight feeling of tenseness in the eyeballs, as if the eyes are turning to follow the train in motion. Let the eyes go and observe how the visual image fades. Relax for about five minutes.

C. Imagine the head of a pin. Note the same experience of tension in the eyeballs as occurred when you imagined a moving object, except now the tension in the eyes is static. Relax the eyes completely. Observe the disappearance of the visual

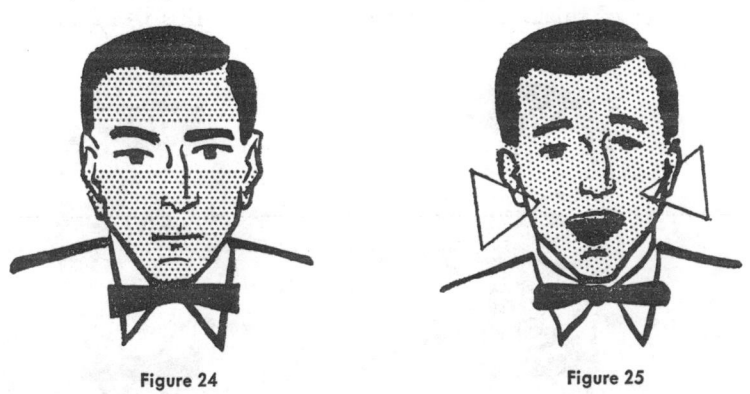

Figure 24

Figure 25

image in the eyes. Devote the remainder of the practice period to complete relaxation.

STEP XV: RELAXING SPEECH

1. RELAXING THE JAWS AND CHEEKS
Practice—two periods

A. Sit in a chair with *eyes open,* head erect. Following ten minutes of relaxation, have jaws meet slightly for about one minute. Note the tension extending from the angle of the jaws to the temples. Let the jaws go and relax for about five minutes.

B. Open the jaws slightly for one minute. Observe the tension in front of the ears (Fig. 25). Let the jaws go and relax for about five minutes.

C. Smile, showing your teeth, for about one minute. Note the tension in the cheeks (Fig. 26). Let the cheeks go and relax for remainder of period.

2. RELAXING THE LIPS AND TONGUE
Practice—two periods

A. Sit in a chair with *eyes open,* head erect. Following ten minutes of relaxation, slightly round your lips in a pout for

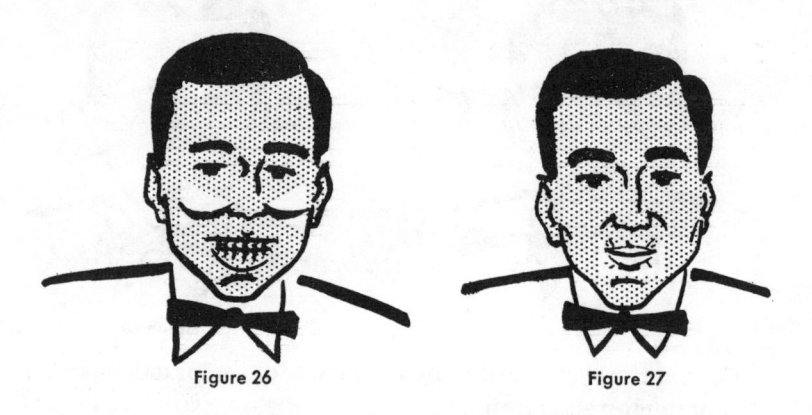

Figure 26

Figure 27

about one minute. Note the tension in the lips (Fig. 27). Let the lips go and relax for about five minutes.

B. Press tongue forward slightly against front teeth for about one minute. Note the tension in the tongue. Let the tongue go and relax for about five minutes.

C. Pull tongue backwards (retract) slightly for one minute. Note the tension in the tongue and in the region behind

Technique of Differential Relaxation

the chin and the floor of the mouth. Let the tongue go and relax for remainder of practice period.

Remember: The ability to relax the tongue is very important.

3. Relaxing the speech apparatus
Practice—two periods

A. In a sitting position with *eyes open,* head erect, relax for ten minutes. Slowly, in a whisper, count from one to ten. Carefully observe the tension in your tongue, lips, jaw regions, throat, diaphragm and all over the chest, as you produce each sound. Relax these parts and note the disappearance of the tension. Maintain a complete relaxed state for about five minutes.

B. Count again to ten in such manner that one cannot see the movement of your lips or hear you make a sound. Observe the tensions in the same regions described in *A*, but they are less intense. Let go all parts and completely relax for about five minutes.

C. Now *imagine* that you are counting from one to ten. Observe the *very faint* sensation of tenseness in the same regions as in *A* and *B*. Bear in mind that during *imagination* and when you are actually counting aloud or whispering, or counting imperceptibly, the sensation of tenseness in the speech apparatus is the same—except for varying degrees of intensity.

Relax the speech apparatus completely—including the muscles of the tongue, lips, jaws, throat, chest and diaphgram. Devote the remainder of the practice period to complete relaxation, letting go all parts that previously received practice.

Remember: Realize that when you speak *in imagination,* you actually talk to yourself.

STEP XVI: RELAXING THE MIND
Practice—six periods

A. Sit in a chair with *eyes open,* head erect. Following ten minutes of relaxation imagine that you are requesting a conductor to let you off a bus. Observe very closely what is now taking place—the instant you begin to think, you have a mental picture, along with slight tension in the eye muscles, as you see the conductor, yourself, and the surroundings where this is taking place. At the same instant, carefully note the slight tension in your speech apparatus.

Relax the muscles of the eye regions (forehead, brow and lids), eyes and the speech apparatus to an extreme degree. Observe that visual imagery disappears and inner speech ceases. *You have stopped thinking.* Maintain such relaxation for ten minutes.

B. Imagine that you are conversing with a sales person while shopping for a pair of shoes. Note the instant faint tenseness in the muscles of your eyes when you visualize the sales person, the shoes and place where this is occurring. At the same instant, observe the experience of slight tenseness in your speech apparatus as you talk to that person. If your reflection includes trying on the shoes, you will also experience faint tenseness *in the feet, as, in imagination, you go through the motions of trying on the shoes.*

Relax the muscles of the eyes and speech apparatus. Observe that visual imagery fades and inner speech ceases as you do so; you have ceased to think! Relax to an extreme degree for the remainder of the practice session.

Remember: 1) Relaxing visual imagery with open eyelids requires skill. With practice you will attain the necessary technique.

2) When you relax the muscles of the eyes and the speech apparatus, you are simply to let

Technique of Differential Relaxation

them go completely in the same manner as relaxing the muscles of the arm or leg, etc.

STEP XVII: EYE RELAXATION DURING ACTIVITIES

1. Partial relaxation of eyes
Practice—two periods

In this lesson you will learn to relax the eyes partially. You have previously learned to let the eyes go completely, so that they are not looking in any direction. However, one cannot continue this with open eyelids for a lengthy period because the eyes will develop a burning sensation, due to the absence of winking and of sufficient moistening of the eyeballs.

Sit in a chair with *eyes open,* head erect. Permit the eyes to wander about to a slight degree. Do not let them relax to an extreme stage. Observe that this results in a moderate amount of winking, prevents discomfort and secures rest for the eyes.

It is advisable for persons who use their eyes a great deal, especially during prolonged reading, writing and close work to rest their eyes in the manner described above. This can be done at frequent intervals, for a few moments, during the day.

2. Relaxing during reading
Practice—two periods

While reading, relax the lower limbs; the back, so far as sitting posture allows; the chest, so far as possible, while inner speech continues; and the arms, so far as is possible, while they hold a book or any reading matter. With extreme relaxation of the forehead and the eyes you will not be able to read. However, relax these parts while holding the reading material in order that you may familiarize yourself with an extreme form of differential relaxation. Now, introduce a slight tension; read the words but keep the eyes and other parts relaxed at the same time. Now you may follow the words but are not able to grasp the meaning due to a still considerable degree of relaxation. Therefore, read again, this time with just enough contractions to get a clear meaning—and no further (Fig. 28).

Figure 28

Remember: Reading while differentially relaxed results in improved efficiency.

9

Release From Worry and Fear

RELEASE FROM the worrying habit requires that you put to practical use the techniques you have learned in your training up to this point.

Included in this chapter is a precise technique to be applied in worry control *at any time—during states of rest or activity*. However, before we enter into this phase of the technique, let us discuss worry and fear in order to better understand these states. Although the literature covering these subjects is vast, we must here limit ourselves to a brief discussion.

As previously pointed out, there are two distinct types of fear—normal and abnormal. For example, when you see a fast-moving automobile bearing down on you, you experience a normal fear—normal, because the object producing the fear is actually there. Other normal fears may be fear of accidents, storms, lightning, fires, and the like—when you are actually endangered by such a phenomenon. When confronted with such dangers you should consider your safety and do something about it. This action results in an abatement and eventual disappearance of the fear so induced. Then all will be well again.

The other type of fear is the abnormal, which is of a pathological nature. This fear (worry) manifests itself in a state of chronic anxiety that terrible things will happen.

We know that life involves certain dangers, and it is foolhardy not to take precautions to evade or confront them. However, to anticipate and worry about these hazards results in useless mental agony.

What action is one to take about problems which can and must be solved? One must first realize that all problems are tension-producing. The individual can choose either to worry excessively about the matter troubling him, using only a part of his intelligence; or he may employ reason, applying his full intellect to the solution of his problem.

Worry does not release, but further augments tension by keeping the irritation constantly in operation. Reasoning helps to solve the situation, but in order to "stop and reason," two things are necessary: first, you must be receptive to reason; second, *before you can reason, you must be relaxed! Furthermore, let it be emphasized that if one is sufficiently relaxed, he will not tend to develop worries in the first place.*

Persons who worry instead of using reason to solve their difficult problems, may be classified as (1) occasional worriers, (2) chronic worriers.

Worry in a Special Situation

There is scarcely a person who has not on one or more occasions been confronted with a critical problem or with a crisis so disturbing that his habitual reasoning reaction has been temporarily lost. Worry under such circumstances is unavoidable. For example, a person dear to you is critically ill. Medical science is doing all it can and you have done everything possible, but so long as the outcome is uncertain, there is bound to be concern and worry. Yet consider the fact that your worry helps neither the patient nor yourself.

Since we live in a world fraught with danger, so long as we are capable of imagination we will worry—unless we acquire a technique for its elimination. At the present time, no other method has been found to meet this problem which is comparable to the therapeutic effects derived from progressive relaxation.

At times the depressing situation must be accepted—"must," because at the time, or in the future, there is nothing that can be done to change matters. If the cause of the worry seems likely to continue or is one of the "unsolvable" problems one encounters occasionally, then the person involved must accept it without undue emotion. If he persists in worrying, he will pass from an acute state of anxiety into a chronic condition of apprehension. When this occurs, worry, fear, and loss of control may dominate almost every waking hour, producing ineffectiveness and a possible breakdown.

Scientific relaxation will enable you to "take it when the going is rough" and "accept the inevitable" with composure.

It should be pointed out that relaxed habits of living are conducive to emotional stability, since the two are synonymous.

Chronic Worriers

Frequently the chronic worrier has no sooner rid himself of one tension-producing problem than he has many others ready to take its place. If he were content to have but one focal problem to worry about, he could find a solution for it and thereby bring an end to the tension-producing situation. But the worries that confuse his mind are countless and therefore insoluble. Such a person is unable to make a rational decision because, being habitually apprehensive, his reasoning processes are impaired.

For instance, there are vast numbers of persons who walk into the physician's office fully convinced that they have heart disease or some other organic illness. Even when medical examination fails to substantiate their fears, they continue to worry needlessly that they are afflicted with such maladies. This is well illustrated in the following excerpts which appeared in the *Chicago Daily News,* February 8, 1956:

"There are more people who think they have heart disease—and don't—than who actually have it, a heart specialist said. . . .

"Dr. Edward Weiss of Philadelphia said these are frequently the most difficult patients to treat.

"They are beset with anxieties and tensions in their personal lives. The heart becomes the focal point because it is the traditional seat of emotions.

"One of the doctor's toughest jobs is to separate the patients who have physical heart disease from those who only fear they do, because they too, develop many of the symptoms—shortness of breath, fatigue, pain in the chest.

"It isn't enough for the doctor to tell the patient that there's nothing wrong with his heart, Dr. Weiss said to a conference for general practitioners, sponsored by the Chicago Heart Association. . . .

"He must try to determine why the patient has the symptoms and help him with his life problems.

"Otherwise the patient's emotional factors will go on to make his life and his family miserable, Dr. Weiss said."

In addition to those who worry about having heart disease, there are countless persons who fear that they have cancer, brain tumor, tuberculosis, and various other diseases. Unfortunately some of these fears may originate from public health education campaigns. Many a cancer phobia may have been induced by a poster with the comforting message, "One out of every five [recently it has been one out of every four] will die of cancer," or, "One out of every twenty of us will be in a mental institution by 1968." These, to name but a few, are the diseases that may strike adults or children if we are to believe statistics. The possible destruction by Fourth of July, Memorial Day and Labor Day accidents also cannot be overlooked. Combine this picture with the new fear of atomic and hydrogen bombs, economic collapse and a possible third world war, and we can appreciate the impact of anxiety in our day-to-day existence.

Release From Worry and Fear

Education of the public in health problems and safety measures is essential to the welfare of the nation and must continue even if it creates anxiety in those individuals with a tendency to worry. Such persons must acquire composure and eliminate the anxieties connected with health warnings and possible destructive eventualities.

STEP XVIII: DIFFERENTIAL RELAXATION OF WORRY

In this step, as an example, the common worry of having heart disease will be presented for you to relax. However, you may substitute any other disturbing mental activity in its place.

Let us assume that while you are engaged in your work or in other activities (social, recreational, etc.) the disturbing thought that you have heart disease is constantly present, despite the assurance of your physician that you do not have the disease. Observe carefully what is taking place while these unpleasant thoughts are present in your mind. You may have mental pictures (most people do) as you visualize the possible fearful effects of having a heart ailment. You have slight tensions in your eye muscles along with sensations as the eyes look at the pictures. The various disquieting images pass before your eyes in the same manner as if they came from a motion picture projector. You are staring at your worry with the eyes strained. In addition there may be also eye movements and persistent frowning.

At the same time note the slight tension in your speech apparatus. Without producing a sound you are talking to yourself or to others repeatedly concerning the issue that is troubling you.

As mentioned in another section of this book, the worry is a secondary activity which interferes with the efficiency of primary activities.

Treatment is to be directed toward the habitual relaxation of tensions that specifically accompany the worrying. The worrier must learn to relax the eyes in order not to review visual impressions of the events connected with heart disease (or any other worry). This can be done in some degree without the eyes being closed, even while one keeps busy in daily affairs. In addition, the speech apparatus must be relaxed in order to do away with inner speech.

Technique

First, relax the forehead, brow and eyelids. At the same instant, relax the eyes and the speech apparatus *completely for a fraction of a second*. Compare what you have just done to shutting off an electric switch. Although this occurs very rapidly, note that when you simultaneously let go the eye regions (forehead, brow and eyelids), eyes and the speech apparatus, even for a fraction of a second, you momentarily stopped the process of thinking and worrying. Actually, the switch upon being shut off eliminated the mental pictures and the inner speech involved in the worry process. *This happens so quickly that in no way has there been an interruption of whatever task you may be engaged in.*

As a result of this relaxation, the secondary activity (worry) has been done away with. You are now to resume your primary activities with differential relaxation as previously instructed.

If the worry reappears, repeat the technique described above and go about your business differentially relaxed.

At the beginning of this new training, relief from the process of worrying may be of short duration. However, with practice and application of the technique, periods free from worry will increase and be more lasting. The end result will be nearly permanent relief from worry.

When the technique of differential relaxation is learned, there will be less tendency to worry, since you will react in

Release From Worry and Fear

lesser degree to aggravating situations. Issues which seemed important during a state of worry will not assume such significance during tranquility.

With habitual relaxation, you will be able to adjust yourself to conditions as they present themselves in everyday living. To be sure, there will be many times when you will perhaps be annoyed by situations you encounter; but with habits of calmness, you will not allow such irritations to render you overemotional and inadequate. You will be able to see things in better perspective, since you will keep in mind the difference between the issue and your reaction attitude. When you worry, your attitude is over-tense. Relax the excess tension present in your various muscle groups, and you will attain peace of mind.

Before we close this chapter, we reiterate that worriers and persons who have overactive minds must take the following into consideration. In daily living, the average person is interested in the matter or content of thought, but not in how he thinks. To rid oneself of worry, the individual must observe what he does when that unpleasant mental process is in operation. The tensions, formerly ignored, will need to be relaxed if the disagreeable thoughts are to be dispelled. Thus in persistent and recurrently disturbing mental activity, the application of scientific relaxation is essential.

10

For Your Heart's Sake— Stop Worrying!

WE SHALL now direct our attention to one of the most dreaded afflictions of modern man—coronary heart disease. The reader will have to study this somewhat technical context, since the facts concerning this malady, in order to be adequately presented, cannot be simplified in the layman's terminology. This disease is dangerous and widespread. The American Heart Association, in advising every adult to resolve to "guard his heart" in 1956, suggested the following New Year's resolution: Learn the facts about the heart and its diseases and avoid needless fears and worry.

To persons who have survived heart attacks, heart specialists offer, in addition to proper diet and medical supervision, the following advice:

1) Avoid fatigue.
2) Cultivate a calm mind.
3) Do not be afraid.
4) Do not worry nor excite yourself.

As mentioned in previous sections in this book, sermonizing in these terms is not sufficient. The patient must receive proper training in relaxation to obtain the necessary results.

In 1772 Dr. Heberden gave the name "angina pectoris" to certain chest symptoms described previously by Dr. Morgagni.

For Your Heart's Sake—Stop Worrying

In 1778 Dr. Jenner associated coronary heart disease with these symptoms, which were more fully described from a clinical angle by Dr. Herrick in 1912.

Angina is characterized by pain in the region of the heart, passing to the left shoulder and the left arm. The blood vessels which carry nourishment to the muscles of the heart itself are commonly called "coronary vessels." It is known that when these vessels become *overtense* and spastic, the heart muscles suffer. This is believed to be the early stage of coronary heart disease. Subsequently these vessels may lose their elasticity, due to hardening. Then the heart becomes less capable of meeting the demands of everyday living, as in digesting large meals, climbing stairs, or walking against a strong wind. When spasticity or hardening deprive the coronary vessels of a blood supply sufficient for increased effort of the heart muscle (so that it can pump effectually to meet the needs caused by the different kinds of exertion), the heart is unable to obtain sufficient oxygen. The pain resulting from this deficiency we call angina.

Since this disease strikes so many persons in the prime of life, it has resulted in much research and an extensive literature. A full theory of coronary heart disease falls into two divisions: (1) physical or physiological, (2) the chemistry and disease involved (chemico-pathological). Investigators have devoted their efforts almost exclusively to the second division. The theory (chemico-pathological) is too complex for the average layman to comprehend and its discussion here will serve no useful purpose. Our interest lies chiefly in a full understanding of the first division.

Studies of the effects of electricity upon living tissue (electrophysiology) give promise of scientific and practical usefulness in the physical (physiological) division. Evidence is accumulating that coronary heart disease is prevalent among persons subject to pressures from occupational sources and/or personality maladjustments. We must keep in mind that the objective obstacles which these people face cannot in themselves lead to heart disability; it is the physiological responses or reactions which bring about functional and organic disorders in the body. Clinical experience indicates that habitual overreaction may result in a variety of other chronic disorders as well. We can affirm that in the process of living, nervous and muscular tensions are indicative of effortful adaptation to environment. This includes not only those efforts which come into play during emotion and during activities of accomplishment, precaution, fear and anxiety, but also those which occur in the midst of the enjoyment of wealth, success and pleasure.

Evidence has been presented in other sections of this book that brain activity and nervous-muscular activity are concomitant and mutually dependent in the human organism as a whole. Mental activities are as dependent upon the muscular system as they are upon the brain, which never acts apart. Various types of recreation do not necessarily entail relaxation of muscles and nerves. Careful measurements have offered conclusive evidence that in overreactive individuals trying to relax by smoking, talking, reading or resting, every muscle attached to the skeleton (voluntary muscles) of the individual may continue to be active instead of really passing into a state of rest. The nerves and muscles do not relax when people participate in sports, such as golf or bowling, or play games like chess or cards. For that reason, it is not sufficient to look for the cause of nervous-muscular tension only in the daily tasks of individuals. One must take into consideration the entire cycle of their living.

Measurements lead to the inference that habitual overactivity of muscles and nerves is widely prevalent among the so-called "healthy" population as well as among those who show signs of coronary insufficiency, high blood pressure, spastic colitis, nervousness and other conditions which may be associated with nervous-muscular hypertension.

A logical approach to this problem is to consider the various factors in modern living as being in some measure responsible for the development of coronary heart ailments in susceptible individuals. It seems improbable that chronic disease processes can ever be entirely comprehended or successfully managed, unless we take the whole human being into account, especially his attempts at adjustments. In physiological terms these attempts involve nervous-muscular activity, the maintenance of which throws excessive loads on the heart and blood vessels (cardiovascular system). This is well recognized in connection with certain types of activity, such as vigorous exercises, which is marked by increased action in the skeletal muscles, heart and lungs. Less apparent, except to the trained observer, is the display of milder nervous-muscular tension which many individuals disclose in business, home, social and other activities. It is unfortunate that modern medical science overlooks and frequently neglects such important features in everyday life, including the signs of overactivity often observable in a great number of patients.

What is not apparent, until disclosed by specialized apparatus that measures and photographs the activity of muscles, is that, at our present tempo of living, individuals can and often do maintain a continuous nervous-muscular activity. In studies made so far, this unnecessary and wasteful action has been found to occur in all occupations. This habitual state, which can be perceived by clinical signs and measured by physiological tests, is called nervous-muscular hypertension (neuromuscular hyperkinesis). If maintained, it has a tendency to drain organic reserves, resulting in the development of states of fatigue.

During periods of high nervous-muscular tension, the many systems of the entire body are of necessity influenced—reflexly, glandularly or via some other mechanisms. As a natural consequence the heart and blood vessels are likewise affected. To maintain persistent contraction in the skeletal muscular system, a sufficient supply of oxygen, glycogen, and other elements, needed for combustion in muscles, has to be furnished.

This supply is provided by the blood stream. At the same time, the products of combustion (carbon dioxide, lactic and pyruvic acids, mineral ash and other waste) must be removed; again the carrier is the blood stream. Such transportation to and from the constantly active nerves and muscles apparently imposes an excessive work burden upon the cardiovascular system. The findings of researchers show that the increased work of the heart, as in muscular exercise, usually entails a moderate increase in arterial pressure. It can be surmised that much of the net effect of chronic nervous-muscular hypertension will be similar on the cardiovascular system. However, this would be less in degree and more or less habitual and constant. The elevated pressure probably will fall short of high blood pressure in persons who are not susceptible to this disease. It is obvious that the entire heart and blood vessel axis becomes relatively overworked under nervous and muscular hypertension in response to the demands of excessive efforts at adjustment.

If coronary heart disease really occurs chiefly in persons who are chronically tense, the question arises whether this link has ever been mentioned by early investigators. Heberden (in 1772), impressed by the symptoms, spoke of "ills justly attributed to the disturbed function of the nerves." In recent years we also find various clinicians (e.g., Ernstene, 1948) stating that attacks of angina pectoris are "induced by exertion or emotion and are relieved promptly by rest or termination of the emotional episode." The same author adds, "One cannot fail to be impressed with the number of stout, emotionally tense, and sensitive individuals who have this [coronary] form of heart disease." Individuals whom Ernstene and other clinicians recognize as emotionally tense and sensitive are the same kind Dr. Jacobson has studied by physiological methods. He has presented specific evidence that these persons show nervous and muscular states marked by prolonged and excessive action potentials, often over their entire skeletal muscle system. Such states he has called neuromuscular hyperkinesis. Physiological studies indicate beyond reasonable doubt that, *with or without attendant emotion, neuromuscular hyperkinesis (1) is characteristic of over-effortful living and (2) in consequence, the heart overworks protractedly with resultant wear and tear manifested in various heart disorders.*

Approximately fifty per cent of all patients afflicted with coronary heart disease are believed also to have elevated arterial blood pressure. It is well known that coronary insufficiency is a prevalent complication in late stages of high blood pressure. Dr. Jacobson found, during states of neuromuscular hypertension, that the blood pressure is relatively elevated even in individuals with normal arteries. It is probable that tension states contribute to the incidence of high blood pressure in those whose blood vessels are deficient in adaptation, both structurally and physiologically. So, in high blood pressure and related disorders, including coronary heart disease, consideration should be given to individual differences due to heredity and to other influences. What may be excessive for the arteries of one person may be easily endured by another. In these disorders, as a rule, women are affected less often and with less severity. *Men are afflicted with coronary heart disease at least four times as often as women, and still more often below the age of forty.* This ratio may be due to hereditary differences, since it has been found by some investigators that in the newly born the average thickness of the inner coat of the coronary arteries is on the average about three times as great in the male as in the female. Furthermore, the thickness increases with age, thus predisposing the male to the disease.

Conditions of "stress" have been studied extensively, chiefly on laboratory animals. Although the interpretations of the investigators differ, they have established that a wide variety of sudden changes results in special activities of glands and hormones. These changes include extensive operations, hemorrhage, burns, exposure to severe heat and cold, and even prolonged and exhausting muscular activity. Under these conditions special hormones are secreted.

The role of so-called "stress" in the development of coronary artery disease is not yet clear. In spite of increasing knowledge, nothing is yet known about the relationship of "stress" effects to those of common daily efforts, which can be studied and measured in the laboratory. We may surmise that with every effort involving contractions of skeletal muscles some degree of "stress effect" is present. However, this is purely an assumption. At the present time, therefore, there is no proof that a direct relationship exists between the chemistry of stress effects and coronary heart disease. It is essential, however, that investigators realize that "stress," as studied up to date, consists of *unusual* changes in the organism, while the phenomena of effort occur every moment and constitute much of one's life.

Even without the presence of chronic high blood pressure, it can be taken for granted that coronary arteries will tend to be overworked if, when, and as the heart itself is subjected to overstrain. Excessive tension of the skeletal muscles is commonly accompanied by an excessive amount of mobility and abnormal tension in the smooth muscle system. Consequently, with coronary heart disease we also find spasticity in the alimentary tract. This naturally involves the colon, small and large intestines and the esophagus. Spasm of the esophagus (gullet) occurs most often in nervous and emotional individuals with or without coronary disease.

In the Laboratory for Clinical Physiology, after approximately daily observation of electrical recordings from muscles of human beings over a period of twenty years, certain generalizations can be made. During states of fear, anxiety or concern, measurement with proper instruments discloses as a rule that no individual muscle attached to the skeleton of the entire body is persistently relaxed. Under such circumstances, the whole organism obviously is in a state of effort, evidently in a form of adaptive behavior. Such internal conditions influence

For Your Heart's Sake—Stop Worrying

hormones and reflexly bring about excessive stimulation of the muscles of the heart and those smooth muscles, including those of the blood vessels. Thus there may be a localized or generalized abnormal tension of arteries and muscles. This increases oxygen consumption.

It has been estimated recently that arteriosclerosis (the thickening and hardening of the walls of an artery) is present in approximately half of the populace of the age of forty or over. From autopsies performed at Bellevue Hospital, A. Wilbur Duryee reports that, of individuals examined, sixty per cent above the age of thirty-five disclosed moderate or advanced arteriosclerosis. As hardening (sclerosis) advances, the nutritive supply from the arterial system upon which the heart work depends responds less to states of *overstrain*. For this reason physicians advise their patients after the age of forty to avoid strenuous forms of athletics such as are advocated for young persons in their twenties.

With advancing age, severe exercise is more likely to produce labored difficult breathing (dyspnea) and other signs of insufficiency. Accordingly, we can understand that under conditions of over-work, strain and/or worry such as are commonly encountered in business and in current affairs, there is an accessory tension upon the glandular, nervous and muscular systems with increased demands upon the circulation in the coronary arteries. *If these conditions resulting in excessive arterial stimulation are extended over months and years; if, in addition, the contracting arterioles lose their youthful capacity to dilate, due to advancing hardening of the coats of the arteries, all that we know of physiology will lead us to expect that spasm of the arteries will develop in some places and that it will tend to become a habit and remain chronic.* That persistent spasm in arteries of human beings can result in hardening of the arteries has long been assumed, but not until recently has this been confirmed in any laboratory animals.

Dr. Edmund Jacobson has this to say in his article entitled,

Principles Underlying Coronary Heart Disease, which I quote in part: "According to the present thesis, the first stage of coronary heart disease is constriction or spasm antecedent to or attended by incipient arteriosclerosis, as the case may be. If the individual fails to be sufficiently careful and engages in the efforts and sub-efforts that mark a strenuous life, the recurrence of coronary spasm becomes inevitable. This may take the form of acute relapse or chronic slight spasm. As is well known, it is impossible by current methods of electrocardiography to determine the presence of coronary disease in approximately 25% of instances, as subsequently diagnosed. Nevertheless we recognize that the employment of electrocardiography has contributed significantly to our knowledge of heart disease. Similarly I do not here propose electro-neuromyometry as capable of determining the imminence of coronary artery disease, although it can be regarded as highly useful as an index of the activities of the individual in whom such disease develops.

"If spasm continues in the coronary arterial system, we can assume that what pathologists call 'wear and tear' will be accelerated. While we do not yet know all the facts which render the individual susceptible to coronary arterial spasm, it is suggested that much can be done for the patient in the light of the physiological principles outlined above. For purposes of preventive medicine, every precaution should be taken to avoid neuro-muscular hyperkinesis and tense states. In my experience sedatives have not proved to be the best means to attain this end. Of greater profit to individuals with habits of chronic neuromuscular tension has been the use of technical methods of instruction to relax. The need for such techniques along with other suitable medical measures obviously is increased once myocardial infarction has appeared. Under such conditions the injured heart is still less able to bear the additional work burden due to excessive neuromuscular tension, which can and often does persist even during the bed-rest commonly prescribed for a protracted period following infarction.

For Your Heart's Sake—Stop Worrying

"In an age often marked by over-specialization, it is common to take sides in a controversy whether coronary heart disease results primarily from faulty fat metabolism or from a faulty way of life. It is important to realize that both sides may be right, for the views are not mutually exclusive. Possibly atherosclerosis is less severe in its effects on the female because of the innate presence and action of female hormones, as suggested by Eilert (and recently by D. P. Barr). As yet it has not been established that any hormone, medication or dietary restriction really retards the development of arteriosclerosis. However hopefully we look to the future of relevant biochemical investigations, we can confidently assume that wear and tear will still continue to take its toll in the human organism, as occurs also with any machine built by man, no matter what agents are discovered for prolonging its existence. In the meantime the heart specialist may well reflect that the life of any instrument depends upon two things: 1) What goes into it and 2) How it is employed. If under the first heading the influences of heredity, fat metabolism, aging and medications are included, there remains to be considered under the second heading the manner of life of any patient. People recognize that the life of any instrument depends upon the care taken of it. Thus from a higher vantage point we can see that life may be prolonged through new developments not alone in the field of biochemistry but also in that of teaching man to take better care of his organism in his daily life."

After reading this chapter, no doubt you will forget some of the technical details. However, by now, you must be aware of the consideration your heart deserves, be it healthy or diseased. This vital organ must not be abused with excessive emotion and exertion. *For your heart's sake, you must learn how to stop worrying.*

GLOSSARY

Action potentials: Sudden sharp changes of electrical potential which signal the activity of some part of the nervous system (also occur in active muscles).

Angina pectoris: Pain and oppression about the heart.

Anxiety: A state of apprehension and fear, without adequate ground accompanied by restlessness and uncertainty.

Arteries: The blood vessels which receive blood from the left ventricle and the aorta and which progressively subdivide carrying the blood to the various parts and organs of the body.

Arteriosclerosis: A degeneration and hardening of the walls of arteries, capillaries, or veins, due to chronic inflammation and resulting in fibrous tissue formation.

Atherosclerosis: Senile type of arteriosclerosis characterized by atheromatous degeneration of walls of arteries.

Autosuggestion: Acceptance of an idea uninfluenced by others that induces mental or physical action or change.

Behavior pattern: A behavior reaction to any given stimulus.

Biochemistry: The chemistry of living things.

Biology: Science of life and living things.

Capillaries: Minute blood vessels.

Cardiovascular: Pertaining to the heart and blood vessels.

Chronic: Long drawn out; applied to a disease that is not acute.

Coronary: Having reference to the arteries which nourish the heart, or veins which receive its waste products.

Diagnosis: Determining the nature of a disease; decision reached after a careful study of symptoms and facts.

Differential relaxation: The absence of an undue degree of contraction in the muscles employed during an act, while other muscles not so needed, remain relaxed.

Electrocardiogram: A graphic record of the variation in time and potential of the electric current associated with action of the heart muscles.
Electrocardiography: The use of a galvanometer or electrometer to obtain a graphic record of the electric currents generated by the beating heart.
Electroneuromyometry: Measurements of electrical currents in nerves and of muscular contractions.
Electrophysiology: Study of electrical activity of and upon living tissue.
Emotional stability: The state of being emotionally mature.
Esophagus: The tube through which food passes from the mouth to the stomach; the gullet.
Etiology: The cause of a disease.

Functional disease: A disease where an organ's function changes but the tissues involved are not altered structurally; opposite of organic disease.
Gastrointestinal system: The organs and parts concerned with digestion and nutrition.
General relaxation: Includes the entire body lying down.
Going negative: Relaxing beyond the point where one seems perfectly relaxed, and even further.

Hyperkinesis: Excessive amount of mobility.
Hypertension: Tension or tonus above normal.

Infarct: An area of tissue deprived of blood.

Metabolism: The successive transformation to which a substance is subjected from the time it enters the body to the time it or its decomposition products are excreted, and by

Glossary

which function of nutrition is accomplished and energy and living substance are provided.

Muscle-sense: The sensation of muscular contraction.

Musculature: The arrangement of muscles in the body or its parts.

Myocardium: The muscular structure of which the heart is almost entirely composed.

Myocardial: Having reference to the myocardium.

Nerve impulse: Name for the excitatory process which travels along a nerve fiber when stimulated.

Nervous system: A system of extremely delicate nerve cells, elaborately interlaced with each other, collectively consisting of the brain, cranial nerves, spinal cord, spinal nerves, autonomic ganglia, ganglionated trunks and nerves, maintaining the vital function of reception and response to stimuli.

With this system belong the sense organs, which are the eye, ear, apparatus for taste and smell, and the skin. The nervous system is divided into two main parts, autonomic and central.

The central nervous system, also known as the cerebrospinal, directs the function of those parts of the brain concerned with muscular activity, consciousness and mental activity, as well as the end organs of all sensory nerves.

The autonomic, also known as the involuntary nervous system, controls the function of the smooth muscles, the heart and the glands. It is divided into two parts, the sympathetic and parasympathetic.

Neuro: Of or pertaining to the nerves or nervous system.

Neuro-muscular: Concerning both nerves and muscles.

Organic disease: A disease affecting the structures of the organs.

Pathology: (1) Study of the nature and cause of disease which involves changes in structure and function. (2) Condition produced by disease.

Pathological: Pertaining to pathology; considered in relation to disease.

Phobia: Any abnormal fear.

Physical disease: A disease affecting the body.

Physiology: The science which deals with the activity of the living body.

Prognosis: Prediction of course and end of disease, and outlook based on it.

Proprioceptive: Noting impulses from afferent nerves in an organism stimulated by its own tissues.

Psychotherapy: Any mental method of treating disease, especially nervous disorders, by means such as suggestion, hypnotism, psychoanalytic therapy, etc.

Residual tension: A fine continued contraction of muscle along with slight movements or reflexes.

Somatic disease: A bodily disease.

Tension-sense: The sensation of muscular contraction.
Therapy: Application of remedies in the treatment of disease.
Thrombosis: Formation of blood clot.

BIBLIOGRAPHY

Bartley, S. *Fatigue*. Baltimore: Williams & Wilkins Co., 1948.
Bartley, S., and Chute, E. *Fatigue and Impairment in Man*. New York: McGraw-Hill Book Co., Inc., 1947.
Binder, J. *Victory Over Fear*. New York: Cowan-McCann, Inc., 1952.
Brams, W. A. *Managing Your Coronary*. New York: J. B. Lippincott Co., 1953.
Cannon, W. B. *Bodily Changes in Pain, Hunger, Fear, and Rage*. New York: Appleton, 1915.
———. *The Wisdom of the Body*. New York: W. W. Norton & Co., 1932.
Chappell, M. N. *In the Name of Common Sense*. New York: Macmillan, 1949.
Coleman, L. L. *Freedom From Fear*. New York: Hawthorn Books, Inc., 1954.
Cowels, E. S. *Don't Be Afraid!* New York: McGraw-Hill Book Co., Inc., 1941.
Dickel, H. A., Dixon, H. H., Coen, R. A., Peterson, R. D. "Fatigue." *Northwest Medicine*, 51:32, Jan., 1952.
Dickel, H. A., Dixon, H. H., Shanklin, J. G., Davidson, G. A. "Observation of the Anxiety Tension Syndrome." *Canadian Medical Association Jour.* 72:1-6, 1955.
Dixon, H. H., Dickel, H. A., Coen, R., Haugen, G. "Tension States: Summary of Etiology, Diagnosis, and Treatment." *Western J. of Surgery, Obstetrics and Gynecology*, 58:667-669, Dec., 1950.
Dixon, H. H., Peterson, R. D., Dickel, H. A., Jones, C. H., West, E. S. "High Energy Phosphates in the Muscles of Depressed and Fatigued Patients." *Western J. of Surgery, Obstetrics and Gynecology*, 60:327-330, July, 1952.
Dixon, H. H., Dickel, H. A., Shanklin, J. G., Peterson, R. D., West, E. S. "Therapy in Anxiety States and Anxiety Compli-

cated by Depression." *Western J. of Surgery, Obstetrics and Gynecology*, 62:338-341, June, 1954.

Dunbar, H. F. *Emotion and Bodily Changes*. New York: Columbia University Press, 1938.

Freeman, G. L. *Physiological Psychology*. New York: Van Nostrand Co., 1948.

Fromm-Reichmann, F. *Principles of Intensive Psychotherapy*. Chicago: University of Chicago Press, 1950.

Gutwirth, Samuel W. *How To Free Yourself From Nervous Tension*. Chicago: Regnery, 1955.

Horney, Karen. *The Neurotic Personality of Our Time*. New York: W. W. Norton & Co., 1937.

Jacobson, E. "On Meaning and Understanding." *Amer. Jour. Psychol.* 22:553-557, 1911.

———. "Use of Relaxation in Hypertensive States." *N. Y. Med. Jour.*, 111:419, 1920.

———. "Reduction of Nervous Irritability and Excitement by Progressive Relaxation." *Jour. of Nerv. and Mental Dis.*, 53:282, 1920.

———. "Treatment of Nervous Irritability and Excitement." *Ill. Med. Jour.*, 39:243, 1921.

———. "The Use of Experimental Psychology in the Practice of Medicine." *Jour. Amer. Med. Assoc.*, 77:342-47, 1921.

———. "The Technique of Progressive Relaxation." *Jour. of Nerv. and Ment. Dis.*, 60:568-78, 1924.

———. "Progressive Relaxation." *Amer. Jour. Psychol.*, 36:73-87, 1925.

———. "Voluntary Relaxation of the Esophagus." *Amer. Jour. of Physiol.* 72:387-94, 1925.

———. "Spastic Esophagus and Mucous Colitis." *Arch. of Int. Med.*, 39:433-45, 1927.

———. "Action Currents from Muscular Contractions during Conscious Processes." *Science*, 66:403, 1927.

———. "Differential Relaxation During Reading, Writing and Other Activities as Tested by the Knee-Jerk." *Amer. Jour. of Physiol.*, 86:675-93, 1928.

_____. "Electrical Measurements of Neuromuscular States During Mental Activities. I. Imagination of Movement Involving Skeletal Muscle." *Amer. Jour. Physiol.* 91:567, Jan., 1930.

_____. II. "Imagination and Recollection of Various Muscular Acts." *Amer. Jour. Physiol.*, 94:22, July, 1930.

_____. III. "Visual Imagination and Recollection." *Amer. Jour. Physiol.*, 95:694, Dec., 1930.

_____. IV. "Evidence of Contraction of Specific Muscles During Imagination." *Amer. Jour. Physiol.*, 95:703, Dec., 1930.

_____. V. "Variation of Specific Muscles Contracting During Imagination." *Amer. Jour. Physiol.*, 96:115, Jan., 1931.

_____. VI. "A Note on Mental Activities Concerning an Amputated Limb." *Amer. Jour. Physiol.*, 96:122, Jan., 1931.

_____. VII. "Imagination, Recollection and Abstract Thinking Involving the Speech Musculature." *Amer. Jour. Physiol.*, 97:200, April, 1931.

_____. "Electrophysiology of Mental Activities." *Amer. Jour. Psych.*, 44:677-94, 1932.

_____. "Electrical Measurement of Activities in Nerve and Muscle" (reprinted from *The Problem of Mental Disorder*. New York: McGraw-Hill Book Co.), pp. 133-45, 1934.

_____. "Electrical Measurements Concerning Muscular Contraction (tonus) and the Cultivation of Relaxation in Man." *Amer. Jour. Physiol.*, 107:230-48, 1934.

_____. "The Course of Relaxation in Muscles of Athletes." *Amer. Jour. Psychol.*, 48:98-108, 1936.

_____. *Progressive Relaxation* (2nd ed.). Chicago: University of Chicago Press, 1938.

_____. *You Can Sleep Well*. New York: McGraw-Hill, 1938.

_____. "The Direct Measurement of Nervous and Muscular States with the Integrating Neurovoltmeter (Action Potential-Integrator)." *Amer. Jour. Psychiat.*, 97:513, 1940.

_____. "Cultivated Relaxation in Essential Hypertension." *Arch. Phys. Ther.*, 21:645, 1940.

_____. "The Physiological Conception and Treatment of

Certain Common 'Psychoneurosis'." *Amer. Jour. Psychiat.*, 98:219, 1941.

———. "The Effect of Daily Rest Without Training to Relax on Muscular Tonus." *Amer. Jour. Psychol.*, 55:248-254, April, 1942.

———. "Cultivated Relaxation for the Elimination of 'Nervous Breakdowns'." *Arch. Phys. Ther.*, 24:133, 1943.

———. "Rest: Physical and Mental." *Ill. Med. Jour.*, 134:2, 1943.

———. "The Cultivation of Physiological Relaxation." *Annals of Int. Med.*, 19:6, 1943.

———. "The Influence of Relaxation Upon the Blood Pressure in 'Essential Hypertension'." *Federation Proceedings*, 6:1, 1947.

———. *You Must Relax*. (3rd Ed.) New York: McGraw-Hill, 1948.

———. "Theory of Essential Hypertension in Man." *Transactions of the New York Academy of Sciences*, Ser. II, Vol. 11, No. 2, Dec., 1948.

———. "Relaxation Methods in Labor." *Amer. Jour. Obstetrics & Gynecology*, 67:1035-1048, May, 1954.

———. "Principles Underlying Coronary Heart Disease." *Cardiologia*, Vol. 26, No. 2, 1955.

Kraines, S. H. and Thetford, E. S. *Managing Your Mind*. New York: The Macmillan Co., 1945.

Liddell, H. S. "The Experimental Neurosis and the Problem of Mental Disorder." *Amer. Jour. Psychiat.*, 94:5, March, 1938.

Liebman, Joshua L. *Peace of Mind*. New York: Simon & Schuster, 1946.

May, Mark A. *Education in a World of Fear*. Cambridge, Mass.: Harvard University Press, 1941.

May, R. *The Meaning of Anxiety*. New York: The Ronald Press Co., 1950.

Menninger, Karl A. *The Human Mind*. New York: Alfred A. Knopf, 1946.

Bibliography

Mikesell, W. H., and Hanson G. *Psychology of Human Adjustment.* New York: D. Van Nostrand, 1952.

Moench, L. G. *Headache.* Chicago: Year Book Publishers, 1947.

Morgan, J. J. B. *The Psychology of Abnormal People.* New York: Longmans, Green and Co., 1936.

———. *How to Keep a Sound Mind.* New York: Macmillan Co., 1952.

Mowrer, O. H. *Psychotherapy.* New York: Ronald Press Co., 1953.

Neufeld, W. "Relaxation Methods in U. S. Navy Air Schools." *Am. J. Psychiatry,* 108:132, Aug. 1951.

Podolsky, E. *Stop Worrying and Get Well.* New York: Bernard Ackerman Inc., 1944.

Rathbone, Josephine L. *Relaxation.* New York: Bureau of Publications, Teachers College, Columbia University, 1943.

Read, G. D. *Childbirth Without Fear.* New York: Harper & Brothers, 1944.

Rees, J. R. *The Health of the Mind.* New York: W. W. Norton & Co., 1951.

Salter, A. *The Case Against Psychoanalysis.* New York: Henry Holt & Co., 1952.

Steckle, L. C. *Problems of Human Adjustment.* New York: Harper & Bros., 1949.

Strecker, E. A. *Fundamentals of Psychiatry.* Philadelphia: J. B. Lippincott Co., 4th Ed., 1945.

Symonds, P. M. *The Dynamics of Human Adjustment.* New York: Appleton-Century-Crofts, Inc., 1946.

Terhune, W. B. "Physiological Psychiatry." *Amer. Jour. Psychiat.,* 106:4, Oct., 1949.

Troland, Leonard T. *The Fundamentals of Human Motivation.* New York: D. Van Nostrand Co. Inc., 1928.

Index

Ability to relax, 24
Activity, relaxation during, 63-76
Adversity, meeting of, 40
Age, and relaxation, 24
American Heart Association, 84
Americans, prone to worry, 10
Angina pectoris, 84, 88
Anxiety, 5, 35, 80
Apprehension, 79
Attitudes, correct application of, 3, 39
Auto-suggestion, avoidance of, 42

Benefits from relaxation, 3, 23

Cannon, Dr. W. B., 12
Charlatanism, appeal to worriers, 7
Children, and mental hygiene, 36
Chronic worriers, 79
Civilization, conducive to worry, 10
Coronary heart disease, 3, 36, 84
Cultism, 7

Determination, 11, 38
Differential relaxation, 17, 63-76, 82
Diseases, created by worry, 5-6
Drugs, use of in worry states, 2, 7, 36, 40

Economic factors, in relation to worry, 1, 10
Education, importance of relaxation in, 36
Efficiency through relaxation, 63-64
Electrical measurement devices used, 15, 33
Emotional thinking, 5
Emotions:
    and blood pressure, 6
    and body disorders, 6
    and colitis, 6
    and heart trouble, 4, 6, 84, 88
    investigations of, 12
    during relaxation, 3, 34
    and sleep, 6
    upsets of, damaging to body function, 6
Energy and relaxation, 64
Environment in relation to worry, 39

Index

Eyes, in thinking and worrying, 13, 15, 17, 55-56, 70-71, 74, 81-82

Fatigue, 6, 23, 64, 87
Fears, effect of, 2, 90
  normal, 2, 77
  pathological, 2, 77
  relaxation of, 61-62, 77, 82
Forebodings, 80
Functional disorders, 7-8, 86

Galton, Francis, and visual imagery, 13
General relaxation, 41-62
Government's responsibility in mental hygiene, 36

Happiness, in relation to relaxation, 1, 9
Harvard University, 12
Headaches, 6
Health and relaxation, 3, 23
Heart disease, coronary, 3, 36, 84
  proper care of, 4, 84, 93
Heart hygiene, 4, 84
High blood pressure, and worry, 6, 36, 89
How to Free Yourself from Nervous Tension, 6, 64

Ill-health, fear of, 80
Imagery, in the process of worrying, 61, 81

Indigestion and worry, 6
Inner speech, in thinking and worrying, 14, 17, 59-61, 73-74, 81-82
Insomnia, 6, 27, 35
  treatment of, 13, 28-29

Jacobson, Dr. Edmund, 9, 12, 13, 14, 15, 17, 33, 88, 89, 91
James, Dr. William, 12

Laboratory for Clinical Physiology, 9, 13, 90
Living, every day, and relaxation, 40

Medical practice, importance of relaxation methods in, 7, 26, 36
Mental activity, and muscles, 15, 34
Mental hygiene, 36
Mind, relaxing the, 60, 74
Modern living, tension of, 10
Muscle sensation, 19, 43
  in thinking and worrying, 15, 34
Muscular contraction, 2, 19
  measurement of, 15, 33

Nerves, overactive, 8
Nervous breakdowns, 10, 36
Nervousness, 35
  treatment through relaxation, 6, 12

Occasional worriers, 78
Organic diseases:
  importance of relaxation in, 9
  prolongation of life, in presence of, 9
Overactive minds, and relaxation, 83
Overactive nerves, 3, 8, 10

Parents, and mental hygiene in children, 36
Pathological fears, 2, 77
Philosophy and relaxation, 37-38
Physical rest, importance of, 26
Physician's diagnosis, importance of, 7-8
Population, importance of education in relaxation methods, 36
Practice in relaxation, 9, 41
Prolongation of life, 9, 23, 35, 93
Progressive relaxation, 13, 22

Quieting the nervous system by means of progressive relaxation, 22

Reality, necessity of facing, 40
Reason vs. worry, 78
Relaxation:
  not a form of exercise, 29-31

Relaxation—*Continued*
  when active, 63-76
  when lying down, 41-62
Residual tension, 19-20, 25
Rest, mental and physical, 2, 24-27

Scientific relaxation, explanation of, 21
Self-discipline, 8, 38
Sleep, 27 (*see also* Insomnia)
Speech apparatus:
  relaxation of, 14, 57-59, 71-73, 82
  in worrying, 61, 81
Stability, emotional, 79
Stress, 37, 89-90

Tension, nervous, 4, 6, 10, 12-13
  meaning of, 19
  relief of, 6, 8, 13, 37, 40, 41-62, 63-76
Tension-sense, 19, 43-45
Thinking, a brain and muscle process, 34, 60, 86
Tragedy, meeting of, 39
Tranquility, quest for, 2, 40

Ulcers, 36
University of Chicago, 13

Visual imagery, during worry, 61, 81

Worrier's common symptoms, 6

Worry:
 chronic, 79
 a cultural disorder, 1
 and disease, 5-6
 occasional, 78
 treatment of, 41-62, 63-74,

Worry—*Continued*
 81-83
Worrying:
 differential relaxation of, 81-82
 general relaxation of, 61-62

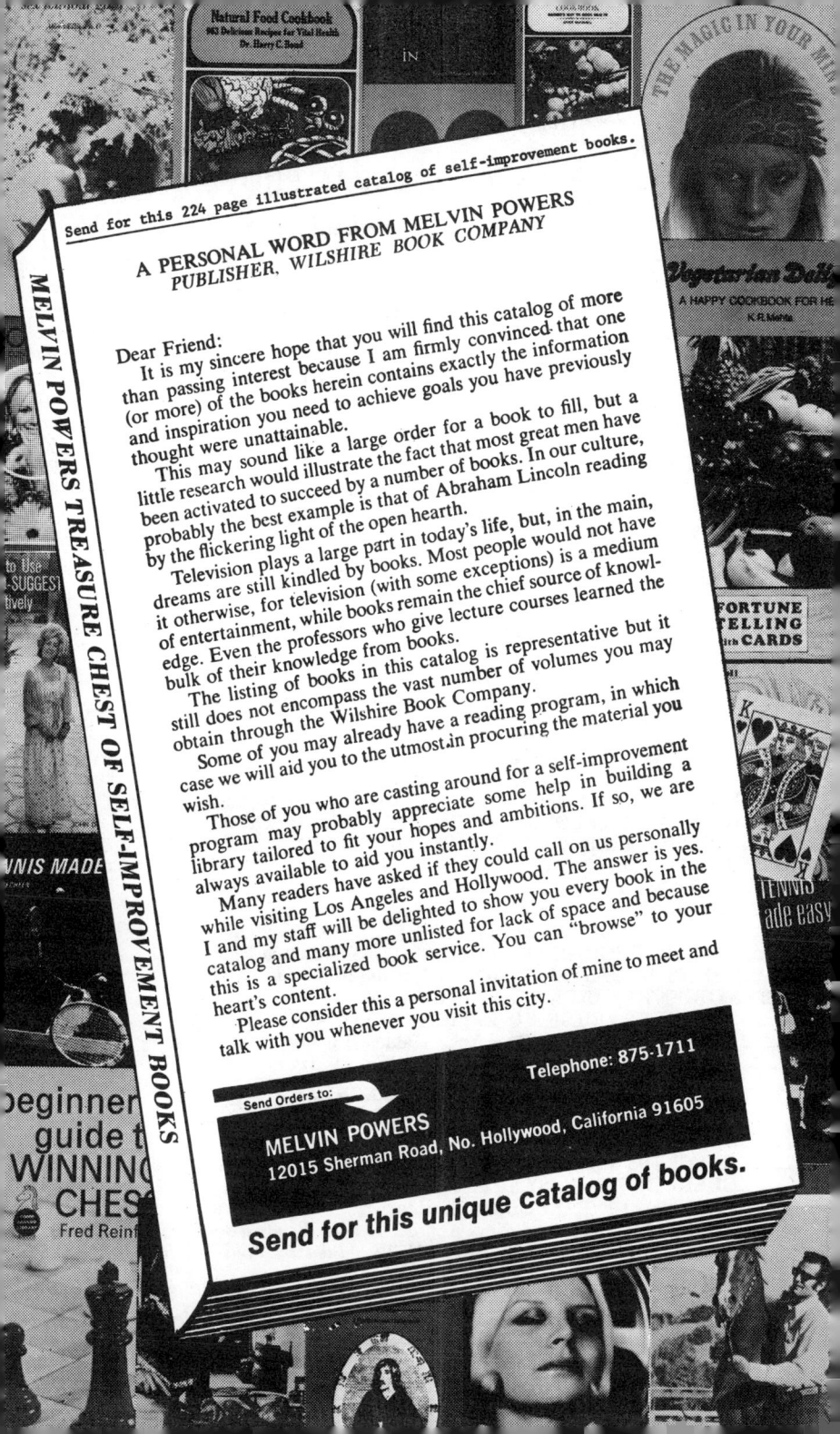

Send for this 224 page illustrated catalog of self-improvement books.

A PERSONAL WORD FROM MELVIN POWERS
PUBLISHER, WILSHIRE BOOK COMPANY

Dear Friend:

It is my sincere hope that you will find this catalog of more than passing interest because I am firmly convinced that one (or more) of the books herein contains exactly the information and inspiration you need to achieve goals you have previously thought were unattainable.

This may sound like a large order for a book to fill, but a little research would illustrate the fact that most great men have been activated to succeed by a number of books. In our culture, probably the best example is that of Abraham Lincoln reading by the flickering light of the open hearth.

Television plays a large part in today's life, but, in the main, dreams are still kindled by books. Most people would not have it otherwise, for television (with some exceptions) is a medium of entertainment, while books remain the chief source of knowledge. Even the professors who give lecture courses learned the bulk of their knowledge from books.

The listing of books in this catalog is representative but it still does not encompass the vast number of volumes you may obtain through the Wilshire Book Company.

Some of you may already have a reading program, in which case we will aid you to the utmost in procuring the material you wish.

Those of you who are casting around for a self-improvement program may probably appreciate some help in building a library tailored to fit your hopes and ambitions. If so, we are always available to aid you instantly.

Many readers have asked if they could call on us personally while visiting Los Angeles and Hollywood. The answer is yes. I and my staff will be delighted to show you every book in the catalog and many more unlisted for lack of space and because this is a specialized book service. You can "browse" to your heart's content.

Please consider this a personal invitation of mine to meet and talk with you whenever you visit this city.

Send Orders to:

MELVIN POWERS
12015 Sherman Road, No. Hollywood, California 91605

Telephone: 875-1711

Send for this unique catalog of books.

Melvin Powers SELF-IMPROVEMENT LIBRARY

ASTROLOGY

_____ASTROLOGY: A FASCINATING HISTORY *P. Naylor*	2.00
_____ASTROLOGY: HOW TO CHART YOUR HOROSCOPE *Max Heindel*	2.00
_____ASTROLOGY: YOUR PERSONAL SUN-SIGN GUIDE *Beatrice Ryder*	2.00
_____ASTROLOGY FOR EVERYDAY LIVING *Janet Harris*	2.00
_____ASTROLOGY GUIDE TO GOOD HEALTH *Alexandra Kayhle*	2.00
_____ASTROLOGY MADE EASY *Astarte*	2.00
_____ASTROLOGY MADE PRACTICAL *Alexandra Kayhle*	2.00
_____ASTROLOGY, ROMANCE, YOU AND THE STARS *Anthony Norvell*	2.00
_____MY WORLD OF ASTROLOGY *Sydney Omarr*	3.00
_____THOUGHT DIAL *Sydney Omarr*	2.00
_____ZODIAC REVEALED *Rupert Gleadow*	2.00

BRIDGE & POKER

_____BRIDGE BIDDING MADE EASY *Edwin Kantar*	5.00
_____BRIDGE CONVENTIONS *Edwin Kantar*	4.00
_____HOW TO IMPROVE YOUR BRIDGE *Alfred Sheinwold*	2.00
_____HOW TO WIN AT POKER *Terence Reese & Anthony T. Watkins*	2.00

BUSINESS, STUDY & REFERENCE

_____CONVERSATION MADE EASY *Elliot Russell*	2.00
_____EXAM SECRET *Dennis B. Jackson*	2.00
_____HOW TO BE A COMEDIAN FOR FUN & PROFIT *King & Laufer*	2.00
_____HOW TO DEVELOP A BETTER SPEAKING VOICE *M. Hellier*	2.00
_____HOW TO MAKE A FORTUNE IN REAL ESTATE *Albert Winnikoff*	3.00
_____HOW TO MAKE MONEY IN REAL ESTATE *Stanley L. McMichael*	2.00
_____INCREASE YOUR LEARNING POWER *Geoffrey A. Dudley*	2.00
_____MAGIC OF NUMBERS *Robert Tocquet*	2.00
_____PRACTICAL GUIDE TO BETTER CONCENTRATION *Melvin Powers*	2.00
_____PRACTICAL GUIDE TO PUBLIC SPEAKING *Maurice Forley*	2.00
_____7 DAYS TO FASTER READING *William S. Schaill*	2.00
_____STUDENT'S GUIDE TO BETTER GRADES *J. A. Rickard*	2.00
_____STUDENT'S GUIDE TO EFFICIENT STUDY *D. E. James*	1.00
_____TEST YOURSELF — Find Your Hidden Talent *Jack Shafer*	2.00
_____YOUR WILL & WHAT TO DO ABOUT IT *Attorney Samuel G. Kling*	2.00

CHESS & CHECKERS

_____BEGINNER'S GUIDE TO WINNING CHESS *Fred Reinfeld*	2.00
_____BETTER CHESS — How to Play *Fred Reinfeld*	2.00
_____CHECKERS MADE EASY *Tom Wiswell*	2.00
_____CHESS IN TEN EASY LESSONS *Larry Evans*	2.00
_____CHESS MADE EASY *Milton L. Hanauer*	2.00
_____CHESS MASTERY — A New Approach *Fred Reinfeld*	2.00
_____CHESS PROBLEMS FOR BEGINNERS *edited by Fred Reinfeld*	2.00
_____CHESS SECRETS REVEALED *Fred Reinfeld*	2.00
_____CHESS STRATEGY — An Expert's Guide *Fred Reinfeld*	2.00
_____CHESS TACTICS FOR BEGINNERS *edited by Fred Reinfeld*	2.00
_____CHESS THEORY & PRACTICE *Morry & Mitchell*	2.00
_____HOW TO WIN AT CHECKERS *Fred Reinfeld*	2.00
_____1001 BRILLIANT WAYS TO CHECKMATE *Fred Reinfeld*	2.00

Melvin Powers SELF-IMPROVEMENT LIBRARY

____1001 WINNING CHESS SACRIFICES & COMBINATIONS Fred Reinfeld 2.00

COOKERY & HERBS

____CULPEPER'S HERBAL REMEDIES Dr. Nicholas Culpeper 2.00
____FAST GOURMET COOKBOOK Poppy Cannon 2.50
____HEALING POWER OF HERBS May Bethel 2.00
____HERB HANDBOOK Dawn MacLeod 2.00
____HERBS FOR COOKING AND HEALING Dr. Donald Law 2.00
____HERBS FOR HEALTH How to Grow & Use Them Louise Evans Doole 2.00
____HOME GARDEN COOKBOOK Delicious Natural Food Recipes Ken Kraft 3.00
____NATURAL FOOD COOKBOOK Dr. Harry C. Bond 2.00
____NATURE'S MEDICINES Richard Lucas 2.00
____VEGETABLE GARDENING FOR BEGINNERS Hugh Wiberg 2.00
____VEGETABLES FOR TODAY'S GARDENS R. Milton Carleton 2.00
____VEGETARIAN COOKERY Janet Walker 2.00
____VEGETARIAN COOKING MADE EASY & DELECTABLE Veronica Vezza 2.00
____VEGETARIAN DELIGHTS — A Happy Cookbook for Health K. R. Mehta 2.00
____VEGETARIAN GOURMET COOKBOOK Joyce McKinnel 2.00

HEALTH

____DR. LINDNER'S SPECIAL WEIGHT CONTROL METHOD 1.00
____GAYELORD HAUSER'S NEW GUIDE TO INTELLIGENT REDUCING 3.00
____HELP YOURSELF TO BETTER SIGHT Margaret Darst Corbett 2.00
____HOW TO IMPROVE YOUR VISION Dr. Robert A. Kraskin 2.00
____HOW TO SLEEP WITHOUT PILLS Dr. David F. Tracy 1.00
____HOW YOU CAN STOP SMOKING PERMANENTLY Ernest Caldwell 2.00
____LSD — THE AGE OF MIND Bernard Roseman 2.00
____MIND OVER PLATTER Peter G. Lindner, M.D. 2.00
____NEW CARBOHYDRATE DIET COUNTER Patti Lopez-Pereira 1.00
____PEYOTE STORY Bernard Roseman 2.00
____PSYCHEDELIC ECSTASY William Marshall & Gilbert W. Taylor 2.00
____YOU CAN LEARN TO RELAX Dr. Samuel Gutwirth 2.00

HOBBIES

____BLACKSTONE'S SECRETS OF MAGIC Harry Blackstone 2.00
____COIN COLLECTING FOR BEGINNERS Burton Hobson & Fred Reinfeld 2.00
____400 FASCINATING MAGIC TRICKS YOU CAN DO Howard Thurston 2.00
____GOULD'S GOLD & SILVER GUIDE TO COINS Maurice Gould 2.00
____HARMONICA PLAYING FOR FUN & PROFIT Hal Leighton 2.00
____JUGGLING MADE EASY Rudolf Dittrich 1.00
____MAGIC MADE EASY Byron Wels 2.00
____SEW SIMPLY, SEW RIGHT Mini Rhea & F. Leighton 2.00
____STAMP COLLECTING FOR BEGINNERS Burton Hobson 2.00
____STAMP COLLECTING FOR FUN & PROFIT Frank Cetin 1.00

HORSE PLAYERS' WINNING GUIDES

____BETTING HORSES TO WIN Les Conklin 2.00
____HOW TO PICK WINNING HORSES Bob McKnight 2.00
____HOW TO WIN AT THE RACES Sam (The Genius) Lewin 2.00
____HOW YOU CAN BEAT THE RACES Jack Kavanagh 2.00

Melvin Powers
SELF-IMPROVEMENT LIBRARY

MAKING MONEY AT THE RACES *David Barr*	2.00
PAYDAY AT THE RACES *Les Conklin*	2.00
SMART HANDICAPPING MADE EASY *William Bauman*	2.00

HYPNOTISM

ADVANCED TECHNIQUES OF HYPNOSIS *Melvin Powers*	1.00
ANIMAL HYPNOSIS *Dr. F. A. Völgyesi*	2.00
CHILDBIRTH WITH HYPNOSIS *William S. Kroger, M.D.*	2.00
HOW TO SOLVE YOUR SEX PROBLEMS WITH SELF-HYPNOSIS *Frank S. Caprio, M.D.*	2.00
HOW TO STOP SMOKING THRU SELF-HYPNOSIS *Leslie M. LeCron*	2.00
HOW TO USE AUTO-SUGGESTION EFFECTIVELY *John Duckworth*	2.00
HOW YOU CAN BOWL BETTER USING SELF-HYPNOSIS *Jack Heise*	2.00
HOW YOU CAN PLAY BETTER GOLF USING SELF-HYPNOSIS *Heise*	2.00
HYPNOSIS AND SELF-HYPNOSIS *Bernard Hollander, M.D.*	2.00
HYPNOSIS IN ATHLETICS *Wilfred M. Mitchell, Ph.D.*	2.00
HYPNOTISM (Originally published in 1893) *Carl Sextus*	3.00
HYPNOTISM & PSYCHIC PHENOMENA *Simeon Edmunds*	2.00
HYPNOTISM MADE EASY *Dr. Ralph Winn*	2.00
HYPNOTISM MADE PRACTICAL *Louis Orton*	2.00
HYPNOTISM REVEALED *Melvin Powers*	1.00
HYPNOTISM TODAY *Leslie LeCron & Jean Bordeaux, Ph.D.*	2.00
HYPNOTIST'S CASE BOOK *Alex Erskine*	1.00
MEDICAL HYPNOSIS HANDBOOK *Drs. Van Pelt, Ambrose, Newbold*	2.00
MODERN HYPNOSIS *Lesley Kuhn & Salvatore Russo, Ph.D.*	3.00
NEW CONCEPTS OF HYPNOSIS *Bernard C. Gindes, M.D.*	3.00
POST-HYPNOTIC INSTRUCTIONS *Arnold Furst*	2.00
How to give post-hypnotic suggestions for therapeutic purposes.	
PRACTICAL GUIDE TO SELF-HYPNOSIS *Melvin Powers*	2.00
PRACTICAL HYPNOTISM *Philip Magonet, M.D.*	1.00
SECRETS OF HYPNOTISM *S. J. Van Pelt, M.D.*	2.00
SELF-HYPNOSIS *Paul Adams*	2.00
SELF-HYPNOSIS Its Theory, Technique & Application *Melvin Powers*	2.00
SELF-HYPNOSIS A Conditioned-Response Technique *Laurance Sparks*	2.00
THERAPY THROUGH HYPNOSIS edited by *Raphael H. Rhodes*	3.00

JUDAICA

HOW TO LIVE A RICHER & FULLER LIFE *Rabbi Edgar F. Magnin*	2.00
MODERN ISRAEL *Lily Edelman*	2.00
OUR JEWISH HERITAGE *Rabbi Alfred Wolf & Joseph Gaer*	2.00
ROMANCE OF HASSIDISM *Jacob S. Minkin*	2.50
SERVICE OF THE HEART *Evelyn Garfield, Ph.D.*	2.50
STORY OF ISRAEL IN COINS *Jean & Maurice Gould*	2.00
STORY OF ISRAEL IN STAMPS *Maxim & Gabriel Shamir*	1.00
TONGUE OF THE PROPHETS *Robert St. John*	3.00
TREASURY OF COMFORT edited by *Rabbi Sidney Greenberg*	2.00

MARRIAGE, SEX & PARENTHOOD

ABILITY TO LOVE *Dr. Allan Fromme*	2.00
ENCYCLOPEDIA OF MODERN SEX &	

Melvin Powers SELF-IMPROVEMENT LIBRARY

LOVE TECHNIQUES *R. Macandrew*	2.00
GUIDE TO SUCCESSFUL MARRIAGE *Drs. Albert Ellis & Robert Harper*	3.00
HOW TO RAISE AN EMOTIONALLY HEALTHY, HAPPY CHILD *Albert Ellis, Ph.D.*	2.00
IMPOTENCE & FRIGIDITY *Edwin W. Hirsch, M.D.*	2.00
NEW APPROACHES TO SEX IN MARRIAGE *John E. Eichenlaub, M.D.*	2.00
PSYCHOSOMATIC GYNECOLOGY *William S. Kroger, M.D.*	10.00
SEX WITHOUT GUILT *Albert Ellis, Ph.D.*	2.00
SEXUALLY ADEQUATE FEMALE *Frank S. Caprio, M.D.*	2.00
SEXUALLY ADEQUATE MALE *Frank S. Caprio, M.D.*	2.00
YOUR FIRST YEAR OF MARRIAGE *Dr. Tom McGinnis*	2.00

OCCULT

BOOK OF TALISMANS, AMULETS & ZODIACAL GEMS *William Pavitt*	3.00
CONCENTRATION—A Guide to Mental Mastery *Mouni Sadhu*	2.00
DREAMS & OMENS REVEALED *Fred Gettings*	2.00
EXTRASENSORY PERCEPTION *Simeon Edmunds*	2.00
FORTUNE TELLING WITH CARDS *P. Foli*	2.00
HANDWRITING ANALYSIS MADE EASY *John Marley*	2.00
HANDWRITING TELLS *Nadya Olyanova*	3.00
HOW TO UNDERSTAND YOUR DREAMS *Geoffrey A. Dudley*	2.00
ILLUSTRATED YOGA *William Zorn*	2.00
MAGICIAN — His training and work *W. E. Butler*	2.00
MEDITATION *Mouni Sadhu*	3.00
MENTAL TELEPATHY EXPLAINED *Hereward Carrington*	.50
MODERN NUMEROLOGY *Morris C. Goodman*	2.00
NUMEROLOGY—ITS FACTS AND SECRETS *Ariel Yvon Taylor*	2.00
PALMISTRY MADE EASY *Fred Gettings*	2.00
PALMISTRY MADE PRACTICAL *Elizabeth Daniels Squire*	2.00
PALMISTRY SECRETS REVEALED *Henry Frith*	2.00
PRACTICAL YOGA *Ernest Wood*	2.00
PROPHECY IN OUR TIME *Martin Ebon*	2.50
PSYCHOLOGY OF HANDWRITING *Nadya Olyanova*	2.00
SEEING INTO THE FUTURE *Harvey Day*	2.00
SEX & HUMAN BEHAVIOR BY THE NUMBERS *Alexandra Kayhle*	2.00
SUPERSTITION — Are you superstitious? *Eric Maple*	2.00
TAROT *Mouni Sadhu*	3.00
TAROT OF THE BOHEMIANS *Papus*	3.00
TEST YOUR ESP *Martin Ebon*	2.00
WAYS TO SELF-REALIZATION *Mouni Sadhu*	2.00
WITCHCRAFT, MAGIC & OCCULTISM—A Fascinating History *W. B. Crow*	3.00
WITCHCRAFT — THE SIXTH SENSE *Justine Glass*	2.00
WORLD OF PSYCHIC RESEARCH *Hereward Carrington*	2.00
YOU CAN ANALYZE HANDWRITING *Robert Holder*	2.00

SELF-HELP & INSPIRATIONAL

ACT YOUR WAY TO SUCCESSFUL LIVING *Neil & Margaret Rau*	2.00
CYBERNETICS WITHIN US *Y. Saparina*	3.00
DOCTOR PSYCHO-CYBERNETICS *Maxwell Maltz, M.D.*	2.50

_____DYNAMIC THINKING *Melvin Powers*	1.00
_____GREATEST POWER IN THE UNIVERSE *U. S. Andersen*	4.00
_____GROW RICH WHILE YOU SLEEP *Ben Sweetland*	2.00
_____GROWTH THROUGH REASON *Albert Ellis, Ph.D.*	3.00
_____GUIDE TO DEVELOPING YOUR POTENTIAL *Herbert A. Otto, Ph.D.*	3.00
_____GUIDE TO HAPPINESS *Dr. Maxwell S. Cagan*	2.00
_____GUIDE TO LIVING IN BALANCE *Frank S. Caprio, M.D.*	2.00
_____GUIDE TO RATIONAL LIVING *Albert Ellis, Ph.D. & R. Harper, Ph.D.*	2.00
_____HELPING YOURSELF WITH APPLIED PSYCHOLOGY *R. Henderson*	2.00
_____HELPING YOURSELF WITH PSYCHIATRY *Frank S. Caprio, M.D.*	2.00
_____HOW TO ATTRACT GOOD LUCK *A. H. Z. Carr*	2.00
_____HOW TO CONTROL YOUR DESTINY *Norvell*	2.00
_____HOW TO DEVELOP A WINNING PERSONALITY *Martin Panzer*	2.00
_____HOW TO DEVELOP AN EXCEPTIONAL MEMORY *Young and Gibson*	2.00
_____HOW TO OVERCOME YOUR FEARS *M. P. Leahy, M.D.*	2.00
_____HOW YOU CAN HAVE CONFIDENCE AND POWER *Les Giblin*	2.00
_____I WILL *Ben Sweetland*	2.00
_____LEFT-HANDED PEOPLE *Michael Barsley*	3.00
_____MAGIC IN YOUR MIND *U. S. Andersen*	2.00
_____MAGIC OF THINKING BIG *Dr. David J. Schwartz*	2.00
_____MAGIC POWER OF YOUR MIND *Walter M. Germain*	2.00
_____MASTER KEYS TO SUCCESS, POPULARITY & PRESTIGE *C. W. Bailey*	2.00
_____MENTAL POWER THRU SLEEP SUGGESTION *Melvin Powers*	1.00
_____ORIENTAL SECRETS OF GRACEFUL LIVING *Boye De Mente*	1.00
_____PSYCHO-CYBERNETICS *Maxwell Maltz, M.D.*	2.00
_____SECRET OF SECRETS *U. S. Andersen*	3.00
_____SELF-CONFIDENCE THROUGH SELF-ANALYSIS *E. Oakley*	1.00
_____STUTTERING AND WHAT YOU CAN DO ABOUT IT *W. Johnson, Ph.D.*	2.00
_____SUCCESS-CYBERNETICS *U. S. Andersen*	2.00
_____10 DAYS TO A GREAT NEW LIFE *William E. Edwards*	2.00
_____THINK AND GROW RICH *Napoleon Hill*	2.00
_____THREE MAGIC WORDS *U. S. Andersen*	3.00
_____TREASURY OF THE ART OF LIVING *edited by Rabbi S. Greenberg*	2.00
_____YOU ARE NOT THE TARGET *Laura Huxley*	3.00
_____YOUR SUBCONSCIOUS POWER *Charles M. Simmons*	2.00
_____YOUR THOUGHTS CAN CHANGE YOUR LIFE *Donald Curtis*	2.00

SPORTS

_____ARCHERY — An Expert's Guide *Don Stamp*	2.00
_____BICYCLING FOR FUN AND GOOD HEALTH *Kenneth E. Luther*	2.00
_____COMPLETE GUIDE TO FISHING *Vlad Evanoff*	2.00
_____HOW TO BEAT BETTER TENNIS PLAYERS *Loring Fiske*	3.00
_____HOW TO WIN AT POCKET BILLIARDS *Edward D. Knuchell*	2.00
_____HOW TO WIN AT THE RACES *Sam (The Genius) Lewin*	2.00
_____MOTORCYCLING FOR BEGINNERS *I. G. Edmonds*	2.00
_____PRACTICAL BOATING *W. S. Kals*	3.00
_____PSYCH YOURSELF TO BETTER TENNIS *Dr. Walter A. Luszki*	2.00
_____SECRET OF BOWLING STRIKES *Dawson Taylor*	2.00
_____SECRET OF PERFECT PUTTING *Horton Smith & Dawson Taylor*	2.00
_____SECRET WHY FISH BITE *James Westman*	2.00
_____SKIER'S POCKET BOOK *Otti Wiedman* (4¼" x 6")	2.50
_____TABLE TENNIS MADE EASY *Johnny Leach*	2.00
_____TENNIS FOR BEGINNERS *Dr. H. A. Murray*	2.00
_____TENNIS MADE EASY *Joel Brecheen*	2.00

WILSHIRE MINIATURE LIBRARY (4¼" x 6" in full color)

_____BUTTERFLIES	2.50
_____INTRODUCTION TO MINERALS	2.50
_____LIPIZZANERS & THE SPANISH RIDING SCHOOL	2.50
_____PRECIOUS STONES AND PEARLS	2.50
_____SKIER'S POCKET BOOK	2.50

WILSHIRE HORSE LOVERS' LIBRARY

AMATEUR HORSE BREEDER *A. C. Leighton Hardman*	2.00
AMERICAN QUARTER HORSE IN PICTURES *Margaret Cabell Self*	2.00
APPALOOSA HORSE *Bill & Dona Richardson*	2.00
ARABIAN HORSE *Reginald S. Summerhays*	2.00
AT THE HORSE SHOW *Margaret Cabell Self*	2.00
BACK-YARD FOAL *Peggy Jett Pittinger*	2.00
BACK-YARD HORSE *Peggy Jett Pittinger*	2.00
BASIC DRESSAGE *Jean Froissard*	2.00
BEGINNER'S GUIDE TO THE WESTERN HORSE *Natlee Kenoyer*	2.00
BITS—THEIR HISTORY, USE AND MISUSE *Louis Taylor*	2.00
BLOND GIRL WITH BLUE EYES LEADING PALOMINO	5.00
(Full color poster 47" x 27")	
CAVALRY MANUAL OF HORSEMANSHIP *Gordon Wright*	2.00
COMPLETE TRAINING OF HORSE AND RIDER *Colonel Alois Podhajsky*	3.00
DOG TRAINING MADE EASY & FUN *John W. Kellogg*	2.00
DRESSAGE—A study of the Finer Points in Riding *Henry Wynmalen*	3.00
DRIVING HORSES *Sallie Walrond*	2.00
EQUITATION *Jean Froissard*	3.00
FIRST AID FOR HORSES *Dr. Charles H. Denning, Jr.*	2.00
FUN OF RAISING A COLT *Rubye & Frank Griffith*	2.00
FUN ON HORSEBACK *Margaret Cabell Self*	2.00
HORSE OWNER'S CONCISE GUIDE *Elsie V. Hanauer*	2.00
HORSE SELECTION & CARE FOR BEGINNERS *George H. Conn*	2.00
HORSE SENSE—A complete guide to riding and care *Alan Deacon*	4.00
HORSEBACK RIDING FOR BEGINNERS *Louis Taylor*	3.00
HORSEBACK RIDING MADE EASY & FUN *Sue Henderson Coen*	2.00
HORSES—Their Selection, Care & Handling *Margaret Cabell Self*	2.00
HOW TO WIN AT THE RACES *Sam (The Genius) Lewin*	2.00
HUNTER IN PICTURES *Margaret Cabell Self*	2.00
ILLUSTRATED BOOK OF THE HORSE *S. Sidney* (8½" x 11½")	10.00
ILLUSTRATED HORSE MANAGEMENT—400 Illustrations *Dr. E. Mayhew*	5.00
ILLUSTRATED HORSE TRAINING *Captain M. H. Hayes*	5.00
ILLUSTRATED HORSEBACK RIDING FOR BEGINNERS *Jeanne Mellin*	2.00
JUMPING—Learning and Teaching *Jean Froissard*	2.00
LIPIZZANERS & THE SPANISH RIDING SCHOOL *W. Reuter* (4¼" x 6")	2.50
MORGAN HORSE IN PICTURES *Margaret Cabell Self*	2.00
PIGEONS: HOW TO RAISE AND TRAIN THEM *William H. Allen, Jr.*	2.00
POLICE HORSES *Judith Campbell*	2.00
PRACTICAL GUIDE TO HORSESHOEING	2.00
PRACTICAL HORSE PSYCHOLOGY *Moyra Williams*	2.00
PROBLEM HORSES *Reginald S. Summerhays*	
Tested Guide for Curing Most Common & Serious Horse Behavior Habits	2.00
RESCHOOLING THE THOROUGHBRED *Peggy Jett Pittinger*	2.00
RIDE WESTERN *Louis Taylor*	2.00
SCHOOLING YOUR YOUNG HORSE *George Wheatley*	2.00
STABLE MANAGEMENT FOR THE OWNER-GROOM *George Wheatley*	3.00
TEACHING YOUR HORSE TO JUMP *W. J. Froud*	2.00
THE LAW AND YOUR HORSE *Edward H. Greene*	3.00
TRAIL HORSES & TRAIL RIDING *Anne & Perry Westbrook*	2.00
TREATING COMMON DISEASES OF YOUR HORSE *Dr. George H. Conn*	2.00
TREATING HORSE AILMENTS *G. W. Serth*	2.00
WONDERFUL WORLD OF PONIES *Peggy Jett Pittinger* (8½" x 11½")	4.00
YOUR FIRST HORSE *George C. Saunders, M.D.*	2.00
YOUR PONY BOOK *Hermann Wiederhold*	2.00
YOUR WESTERN HORSE *Nelson C. Nye*	2.00

The books listed above can be obtained from your book dealer or directly from Wilshire Book Company. When ordering, please remit 20c per book postage. Send for our free 224 page illustrated catalog of self-improvement books.

Wilshire Book Company
12015 Sherman Road, No. Hollywood, California 91605

Notes